HOW to DRESS AN EGG

How to Dress an Egg

Surprising and *Simple* Ways to COOK DINNER

Ned Baldwin *and* Peter Kaminsky

Photographs by HIRSHEIMER & HAMILTON ✱ *Illustrations and Hand Lettering by* GERARDO BLUMENKRANTZ

A Rux Martin Book
HOUGHTON MIFFLIN HARCOURT
Boston • New York 2020

hmhbooks.com

Library of Congress Cataloging-in-Publication Data
Names: Baldwin, Ned, author. | Kaminsky, Peter, author. | Hirsheimer, Christopher,
photographer. | Hamilton, Melissa, photographer.
Title: How to dress an egg : surprising and simple ways to cook dinner / Ned Baldwin,
Peter Kaminsky ; photographs by Hirsheimer & Hamilton ; illustrations by Gerardo Blumenkrantz.
Description: Boston : Houghton Mifflin Harcourt, 2020. | Includes index.
Identifiers: LCCN 2019040521 (print) | LCCN 2019040522 (ebook) | ISBN 9781328521835 (hardback)
| ISBN 9781328521842 (ebook)
Subjects: LCSH: Dinners and dining. | Cooking (Natural foods) | Cooking (Eggs)
| LCGFT: Cookbooks.
Classification: LCC TX737 .B383 2020 (print) | LCC TX737 (ebook) | DDC 641.6/75—dc23
LC record available at https://lccn.loc.gov/2019040521
LC ebook record available at https://lccn.loc.gov/20190405

Book design by RAPHAEL GERONI

Printed in China

SCP 10 9 8 7 6 5 4 3 2 1

To me, cooking is an art form, and like any art form, you first have to learn the fundamentals. And then, once they're there, once they're just part of you, and you get up and do a little dance or something, you don't follow somebody else's formula. You can take off on your own, and you learn through doing. Then you can let go of some of these strict rules and make your own rules.

—JUDITH JONES

Eater (September 23, 2015)

For Jordana, Hazel, and Irving

THANKS FROM THE CHEF

JAY MOSKOWITZ, who taught me that if I don't like something, I probably haven't had it cooked properly.

SCOTT CARSBERG, who showed me that I can make art that people put in their bodies.

TODD GINSBERG, who opened the door to the professional kitchen.

GABRIELLE HAMILTON, for turning an insecure artist into a confident egg cook.

CHRIS PAVONE, for his invaluable advice on the art and practice of cookbook making.

The wonderful people of Orient, New York, who encouraged me to do what I thought I couldn't.

KitchenAid
COSORI

Contents

BASICALLY SPEAKING

I know this to be true: If you can learn to cook one thing well and make a recipe truly your own, you will have opened the door to creating a lifetime's worth of recipes. Once you can conjure up the springy, juicy explosion of a crispy roasted chicken, the silky delicacy of a poached cod fillet, or something as deceptively undemanding yet completely satisfying as a boiled egg, you will have the building blocks for home cooking that satisfies and delights. Simply stated, the idea behind this book is to showcase the variety, nuance, and pleasure that can be had by mastering a simple technique and then going down the delicious paths where imagination leads you.

In the chapters that follow, I've shined the spotlight on twenty main ingredients—from steak to salad, lamb to leeks, eggplant to eggs—and given you a simple and foolproof (well, reasonably foolproof) basic recipe. Each basic recipe is accompanied by a handful of variations, and that's where a lot of the nuance and style in my cooking (or anybody's) come to life. It has taken me years behind the stove of a busy restaurant, when it's firing on all cylinders, to hone these basic recipes to their uncomplicated essence. Often they require little more than some salt and a bit of oil or water. No special equipment needed—just some knives, pots and pans, your stove, and a healthy appetite.

Having a restaurant and customers willing to try new things has given me a dream laboratory for trying out new recipes—whether they come from the mysterious grace of inspiration, from tantalizing ideas I pick up from the many cookbooks that are always stacked on my night table, or from the bubbling cauldron of ideas that flow from living, working, and traveling in a food-crazed era.

I often tell people I am a home cook who became a restaurant chef who remains a home cook at heart. I even named my restaurant Houseman in honor of home cooking. In the years spent perfecting my style, I have learned a few lessons that any home chef can use in their cooking. First, whenever possible, make things in the shortest amount of time that is practical. For example, I've found that I can roast an average-sized chicken in less than half an hour (page 26) or cook an eggplant (page 158) in under than 10 minutes. Second, minimize the actual amount of attention you need to pay to the recipe. Case in point: When poaching cod (page 90) or shrimp (page 114), I bring water to a boil, turn the heat down (or off), add the seafood, set a timer, and busy myself with preparing the rest of the meal. For slow-cooking recipes that require minimal mental bandwidth (see the chapters on beets, pork shoulder, leeks, and carrots), I put the main ingredient in a pot with a splash of oil and salt (not even that for beets), seal the pot with aluminum foil, place the lid on top, and cook in a low-temperature oven for a long time.

CONTINUED

You'll notice that practically all the recipes are served family style. Serving food this way, in addition to being easier and less fussy, delivers a message of generosity. A big platter of food allows everyone at the table to dig in and share. It is, in a fundamental sense, a form of communion.

Still, it all gets back to the basics. As you go through this book, I urge you to make the basic recipes a few times and nail them down before moving on to the variations. This book—or any book—can tell you what to do, but only repetition and practice in the kitchen will tell you how a recipe feels: its smells, its touch, even its sounds. Hands-on experience will help you make the adjustments that your stove, your pans, and your palate require. Almost all of the dishes here can be served as is—often with nothing more than a squeeze of lemon, a splash of oil, or a dash of salt. Once you have the fundamentals under your belt, the variations become adornments on an already beautiful creation. And in a short while, you will be able to take your tastes and inclinations into your own recipes. They are waiting to be born. I promise.

Fig. 1
Fig. 2
Fig. 3

First Things First

PREPPING

Your cooking will be much less stressful (and much more rewarding) if you get all the chopping and slicing of ingredients done before you start working your way through a recipe. Once things are cooking, you don't want to have to stop to prep other ingredients. Much better to do it before you cook. And it's easier to follow a recipe without constant interruption. Having a lineup of little bowls at the ready—each with one ingredient or a mixture—goes a long way toward ensuring success. By making certain things ahead—like toasted nuts, flavored oils, spice mixes, and croutons—I always have ingredients on hand to add texture, aromas, and flavor that can transform a basic recipe into something more exciting yet not very complicated.

PLEASE TASTE

I'm a firm believer that the human palate, which evolved over millions of years to seek out good tastes, is a much better tool for assessing flavor than a list of gram-accurate quantities of ingredients on a page. The best cooks always taste their food from start to finish. They try the raw ingredients, the semi-cooked ingredients, the herbs, the butter, the vinegar, the oil. They taste partly out of curiosity and partly because it's fun. Taste everything you cook while you're cooking it, from the beginning right up to the end. How else will you know what you're doing?

NO DICE

In my early years in professional kitchens, I diced countless tons of vegetables into teeny, tiny cubes. However, in my own restaurant, we don't do that, and I don't ask you to in this book either. A good kitchen knife and the knife skills you already have will carry you through all of my recipes.

HOW I MEASURE

Can you have too much of a good thing? When it comes to fresh herbs, I think not. I love fresh herbs, and I use an abundance of them in my recipes. For me, herbs are seldom relegated to supporting-actor status. In fact, they are often the costars of the show. When I measure, I use the leaves and the small stems that come off the main branch of a sprig; these slender offshoots are tender and flavorful. I pack the herbs into a measuring cup, brimful and overflowing, then chop or mince them if my recipe calls for that. It's not a precise way of measuring, and I'm fine with that. Rough measurements are fine. Err on the side of more rather than less.

How Much Salt?

People like different degrees of saltiness. Each person's appetite for salt is subjective. In this book, I aim a bit low for my taste because of the old adage: *You can always add salt, but you can't take it away.* So, take my advice with a grain of salt and taste your food as you go.

STARTING COLD

I always advocate putting the oil or butter in a cold pan and allow it to heat up before adding other ingredients. If you put a pan with nothing in it over a hot burner, there are no visual cues or smells that tell you how hot the pan is. However, if you put oil or butter in a cold pan, it will tell you all sorts of things as it gets hot; its viscosity (thickness) changes, it moves differently in the pan, it shimmers, it smokes, it produces aromas. This is all valuable sensory information. So don't wait until a pan is hot to add the oil or butter to it. Put it in at the start when the pan is still cold.

TAKING THE TEMPERATURE

Thermometers

Taking the internal temperature with an instant-read thermometer is much more reliable than guesswork when you are roasting a chicken or cooking a steak or anything that requires a reasonably accurate temperature for judging doneness.

A laser thermometer is invaluable for checking the temperature of the oven before baking, roasting, frying, slow-cooking, or braising. These thermometers are not very costly—about twenty bucks. I also use a laser thermometer to check the temperature of oil or water heating in a pot on the stove. That way, I can easily tell when a pot of water reaches, say, the ideal poaching temperature of 160°F or when oil for frying hits the crust-creating sweet spot of 350°F.

Some Go-To Ingredients, Always on Hand

TOASTED SEEDS *and* NUTS

Toasted seeds and nuts are among my fundamental pantry items. I add them to everything from a salad to a cake to a roasted fish. I prefer to fry most seeds and nuts in oil rather than roasting them dry in the oven. Frying in oil produces uniform crispness. As the nuts or seeds fry, they infuse the oil with their flavors, so when you're done, you have both toasted nuts and nut-flavored oil. I store the oil in the refrigerator, which helps preserve its flavor.

1 cup unsalted nuts or seeds
2 cups canola or grapeseed oil
Kosher salt

Combine the nuts or seeds and oil in a small pot and set over medium-high heat. Set a strainer over a heatproof bowl and keep nearby. Stir the nuts or seeds as the oil gets hot so that everything cooks through at the same rate. Continue stirring, adjusting the heat as necessary so the nuts or seeds fizz and gently bubble in the oil. The tiny bubbles are water escaping from the nuts or seeds, making them crunchier. When they are ready (3 to 7 minutes, depending on size; see page 18 for visual cues), they will smell toasty. Carefully pour the nuts or seeds and oil into the strainer, then spread the drained nuts or seeds on a plate lined with a paper towel. Season lightly with salt to taste. Let the oil cool, then refrigerate. Store the nuts or seeds separately.

TOASTING SEEDS AND NUTS IN THE OVEN

If you're more comfortable toasting seeds and nuts in the oven rather than frying them in oil, that's fine. The cooking time will vary depending the size of the seed or nut, but regardless of their type, toast them in a 325°F oven.

Spread the seeds or nuts on a baking sheet in a single layer so they toast evenly and slide them into the oven. Start checking after 10 minutes, then continue to check at 3-minute intervals, until the seeds or nuts darken in color and emit a wonderful toasty smell.

TOASTED MIXED SEEDS

To finish salads and cooked vegetables, I always have a supply of mixed toasted seeds for crunch, flavor, and an interesting accent.

⅓ cup pumpkin seeds, toasted (page 17)
2 to 3 tablespoons sunflower seeds, toasted (page 17)
1 tablespoon sesame seeds, toasted (page 17)
1 teaspoon nigella seeds (sometimes called black onion or black cumin seeds; optional, but I love them)

Combine the seeds and keep around.

SOME VISUAL CUES FOR TOASTED NUTS AND SEEDS

ALMONDS are sold roasted; raw with the skin on; blanched, skin off; slivered; or sliced. I mostly use skin-on raw almonds, but you can avoid a lot of chopping if you buy slivered or sliced almonds. It's up to you. In any case, when almonds are toasted, the nut meat turns from ivory to light khaki. Even when they are sold roasted, almonds usually benefit from a little more time in hot oil or in the oven.

HAZELNUTS are sold both skin on and skin off. I always buy blanched, skin-off nuts. I usually crush them with the flat of a knife before frying. A toasted hazelnut takes on a light honey color, with a few golden spots. If you can only find hazelnuts with the skin on, the great baker Alice Medrich once showed Julia Child how to skin them quickly: Bring 2 cups water to a boil in a small pot, add 3 tablespoons baking soda and 2 cups nuts, and boil for 3 to 5 minutes, until the water turns black. Drain the nuts in a strainer and cool under cold running water. The nuts should slip easily out of their skins when you pinch them. Dry them well on paper towels.

PISTACHIOS will show patches of gold, pale green, and cedar brown. You may find they toast faster than other nuts.

GREEN PUMPKIN SEEDS (PEPITAS) go from deep green to pale green with mahogany blushes.

SESAME SEEDS are available already roasted, and I'm fine with that—go ahead and take the shortcut. If you have untoasted seeds, however, they can go straight onto a baking sheet and into a 375°F oven, no oil necessary. Check at 4-minute intervals, giving the pan a shake each time. If you see a bit of color, set the timer for 2 more minutes. It's important to use a timer: Speaking from experience, it's easy to forget that the seeds are in there until you smell them burning, and by then it's too late.

SUNFLOWER SEEDS will turn from a dull gray to a light mahogany.

HERB-INFUSED OILS

When I have extra fresh thyme, rosemary, sage, or savory, I like to infuse grapeseed or canola oil by warming the herbs in the oil and letting them steep for a while.

1 bunch fresh herbs (10 to 20 sprigs)
1 ½ cups canola or grapeseed oil

Put the herbs and oil in a medium saucepan and gently heat the oil to 140°F to 160°F. Remove from the heat and let steep for 40 minutes. Strain the oil before storing. It will keep, covered and refrigerated, for at least 2 weeks.

OIL-POACHED GARLIC *or* SHALLOTS

When cooked for a long time in oil at a low temperature, garlic and shallots undergo a magical transformation. I use them all the time.

15 garlic cloves, peeled; or 3 to 4 medium shallots, thinly sliced
2 cups canola or grapeseed oil

Preheat the oven to 225°F.

Put the garlic or shallots in a small ovenproof saucepan and add the oil. Place in the oven.

Check after 45 minutes; if the garlic or shallots mash easily with a fork, they're done. If not, set your timer for another 15 minutes and keep at it until the garlic or shallots are very soft. Let cool, then store in the refrigerator. The garlic or shallots should keep well in the oil for a few weeks, which is far beyond the time it will take for you to use them up if you make them part of your cooking.

QUICK OIL-POACHED GARLIC *or* SHALLOTS

Here's a quicker version of oil-poached garlic if you're in a rush.

1 garlic head or large shallot, broken into cloves and peeled
½ cup vegetable oil
3 tablespoons water
½ teaspoon kosher salt

Slice the garlic cloves or shallots ⅛ inch thick.

Combine the garlic, oil, water, and salt in a small saucepan set over medium heat. As soon as the oil bubbles, 2 to 3 minutes, turn the heat to low. Cook for another 11 to 13 minutes, until the garlic or shallot has softened so you can mash them between your fingers.

Store in a covered container in the fridge for up to a week.

BASIC MAYO

Fluffy and light, mayonnaise is the uncredited fourth ingredient in the world's most beloved sandwich: the BLT. It caresses the lettuce, provides a savory frosting on bacon's crispy edges, and slicks the tangy tomato. Among its many virtues, you can infuse the mayo with whatever flavors strike your fancy: lemon, chipotle, basil—the sky is the limit. However, the first step is to learn how to make it in its bare-bones simplicity. It always starts with oil, egg yolk, and a liquid with a high water content, such as lemon juice or vinegar (water itself is just fine too).

1 large egg yolk
2 tablespoons water, fresh lemon juice, or vinegar
Pinch of kosher salt
1 cup vegetable oil

Combine the yolk, water or other liquids, and salt in the bowl of a food processor; turn it on and let run until the ingredients are combined, about 30 seconds. Open the lid and make sure there's no egg left uncombined; if there is, scrape it into the rest of the matter with a rubber spatula, turn the food processor on, and let it run for another 30 seconds. With the processor running, drizzle in about a tablespoon of the oil (you can eyeball it), and then process for 10 seconds. Gradually drizzle in the remaining oil, then scrape down the sides and run the processor for another 15 seconds. Scoop the mayo into a lidded container and store in the fridge. It's good for about 3 days.

CRUNCHY CROUTONS

As the cartoonist Nathan W. Pyle wrote, "Croutons are a great comeback story when you think about it. Bread no one ate yesterday becomes the best part of the salad today." I like them in all sizes, depending on the recipe. Some as small as cherries, others as large as plums. In every case, the recipe is as follows.

About 20 pieces of bread torn from a loaf of rustic sourdough or rye (crust removed)
3 to 4 tablespoons olive oil
Kosher salt

Preheat the oven to 350°F.

Toss the bread pieces thoroughly with the oil, shower with salt, and spread on a baking sheet. Slide into the oven. Check on the croutons after 10 minutes; they may have to go longer.

BROWN BUTTER MAKES IT BETTER

Golden and caramelly, brown butter is equally at home in savory and sweet recipes. I crave it basted over steaks or vegetables, combined with lemon and herbs over fish, or whisked into crepe batter. I also like to fry nuts in it, then keep any leftover extra-flavorful brown butter in the fridge.

It's helpful to have an idea of what's happening as the butter goes from pale yellow to brown, not least of all so you can avoid burning: As the butter gets hot, the water in it turns to steam, causing the butter to foam. The foam recedes when the water has cooked out, leaving milk fat and milk solids. The solids are the little particles that, left to their own devices, fall to the bottom of the pan. They'll brown in the fat but can burn eventually, which is why once the butter foams, it's important to keep the solids and fat moving so that everything cooks evenly.

4 tablespoons (½ stick) unsalted butter

Put the butter in a small saucepan and place over medium-high heat. Once the butter foams, continuously swirl the pan for even browning and to prevent the milk solids from burning. You are looking for a golden brown color. The butter will have a sweet, nutty smell. This process should take roughly 4 minutes. Pour the butter into a bowl, brown bits and all. The butter will keep for 1 to 2 weeks in the refrigerator or up to 6 months in the freezer.

PRESERVED LEMONS

Very common in the Middle East and North Africa, preserved lemons have yet to be fully embraced in this country. They are a superb and long-lasting condiment that adds salt, acid, and floral notes. They are excellent in salads or slaws and on cooked vegetables, fried fish, roast chicken, and lamb. They are also easy to make. All you need is salt and 4 or 5 lemons, and you'll be good for months.

4 or 5 lemons
Kosher salt

Stand each lemon on end and slice downward most but not all the way through it. Give the lemon a quarter turn and slice it again the same way. You can now pry open the lemon so that the flesh is exposed. Add ½ inch of salt to the bottom of a quart container. Pour salt into each lemon and place in the container. Top off with more salt. The lemons will be ready in 2 weeks; every so often, invert the container a few times so that salt and the juice that leaches out of the lemons flow over everything. You'll know they're ready when the pith is translucent and the rind has softened. It's only the rind that you will use in recipes. Preserved lemons will keep for up to 6 months in the fridge.

HOW TO MAKE LOVE FROM SCRATCH

ROAST CHICKEN

ROAST CHICKEN

BASIC RECIPE

I can get a raw chicken from fridge to table in under thirty minutes by taking advantage of a skillet on the stovetop to start. Then I resort to a rarely, if ever, used part of the oven—the floor. In most ovens, the heat comes from a burner or heating element underneath a metal sheet on the bottom of the oven. The oven bottom acts as a diffuser and functions as a burner underneath the skillet, allowing the skin to continue to crisp while the ambient air temperature of the oven roasts the bird. The only part of the bird that ever needs to touch the pan is the skin side. The skin acts as a barrier between the tender, moist flesh and the hot cast-iron pan. Me, I'm not too fussy about how the interior of my oven looks, but be forewarned that over time this foolproof technique might scuff the oven floor a little.

I remove the backbone as well as the ribs and breastbone before cooking the chicken. This speeds the cooking and makes it easier to slice the breast meat. You can make the chicken without doing this, but it will take longer. Deboning the breast gets the best and quickest results. If you don't know how, ask the butcher to do it for you (supermarkets are often happy to oblige). Failing that, you can butterfly the chicken at home (this is also known as a spatchcoked chicken). To do it yourself, remove the backbone by cutting down along both sides of it with a pair of kitchen shears (don't worry about the ribs and breastbone). After removing the backbone, lay the chicken skin side down on a cutting board and press down hard to flatten it.

SERVES 4

PREP THE CHICKEN

1 organic chicken (2½ to 3 pounds), butterflied and, if possible, breast bone and ribs removed
1½ tablespoons kosher salt
A few tablespoons canola or grapeseed oil
A lemon wedge or two (optional)

Salting the chicken in advance ensures that the seasoning is evenly distributed throughout the meat. This method results in meat with salt in it rather than on it.

Put the bird in a large metal bowl, sprinkle the salt evenly all over it, and rub the chicken around the inside of the bowl until all the salt adheres.

Note: Food geeks like me with a gram scale will find that a 2½-pound chicken, after deboning, weighs 1,134 grams. Depending on your taste for salt, you'll need between 1.1 percent and 1.4 percent of the chicken's weight in salt (12.5 to 15.8 grams).

Let the salted chicken rest in the fridge for at least 2 hours before cooking; the chicken is good to go for at least 24 hours after salting.

DRY THE CHICKEN AND HEAT THE OVEN

About ½ hour before roasting the chicken, turn the oven to 475°F and let it heat up (this may take a while). You want it plenty hot in there. Meanwhile, take the chicken from the fridge and pat dry with paper towels. Set aside.

COOK THE CHICKEN

Oil a large heavy-bottomed skillet; cast iron is my favorite. (If your skillet won't accommodate the whole chicken, split it into 2 halves and use two skillets.) You want a thick coating of oil (more than a slick, less than a puddle). Place the pan over a high heat on the stovetop until you see the faintest wisp of smoke rising from the oil. Gently—*really gently*, so the oil doesn't splatter and burn you—lay the chicken in the pan skin side down. Lower the heat to medium-high and cook until the skin turns faintly blond, about 3 minutes.

Transfer the skillet to the floor of the oven.

Depending on the size of the bird and whether it is deboned or just butterflied, the total cooking time in the oven will range from 18 to 30 minutes. The chicken is done when the temperature in the thickest part of the thigh registers 155°F to 160°F on an instant-read thermometer.

When the chicken is done, cut it into manageable pieces, put them on a platter, and serve as is, or with a squeeze or two of lemon.

DONENESS

People get a little nutty when it comes to chicken and doneness. We give timing guidelines in the recipe here, but it could be more, could be less, depending on the weight of the chicken, the type of pan you use, the heat in your oven, the fickle kitchen gods, and whether your soul is pure. My test is to insert a skewer or cake tester into the thickest part of the thigh and check for clear juices to seep out—that means it's cooked through; the skewer should also feel quite hot to your lip. But the skewer test takes some getting used to, and you have to cook a lot of chickens before it becomes second nature. Or, you can just use an instant-read thermometer.

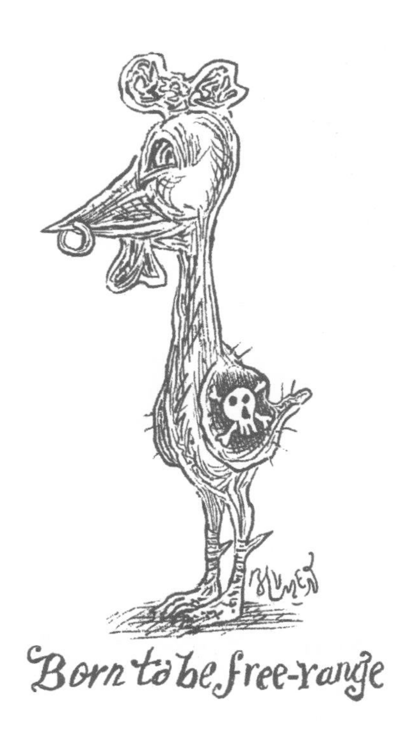

SPRINGTIME CHICKEN *with* HERB SAUCE

Right around Easter, when I walk outside in shirtsleeves for the first time in months and the crocuses and daffodils are popping, I find myself craving green: peas, asparagus, fresh lettuces. Alas, in the Northeast, the farms and fields are still discouragingly barren; it's always at least another month before good local fresh produce hits the stands. In the meantime, I head to the market and grab whatever herbs look best, then whip up a bright pan sauce with the herbs, anchovies, capers, garlic, and crushed red pepper flakes. There's no butter in this recipe, but thanks to the mighty emulsifying powers of Dijon mustard, the sauce comes together in a satisfyingly creamy way. Serve with Soft Leeks (page 182), if you like.

SERVES 4

PREP THE CHICKEN

1 organic chicken (2½ to 3 pounds), deboned or butterflied (see basic recipe, page 26)
2 to 3 teaspoons kosher salt

Salt the chicken and refrigerate it as directed on page 26.

MEANWHILE, MAKE THE CROUTONS

20 cherry-sized pieces torn country bread (crust removed)
3 tablespoons olive oil
Kosher salt

Preheat the oven to 350°F.

Toss the bread pieces thoroughly with the oil, shower with salt, and spread on a baking sheet. Bake for 10 to 15 minutes, until the croutons have crisped. Set aside.

PREP THE SAUCE

6 anchovy fillets, minced
6 capers, minced
1 tablespoon minced fresh marjoram or rosemary
1 tablespoon minced Oil-Poached Garlic (page 20), mashed
3 tablespoons oil from Oil-Poached Garlic (page 20) or olive oil
Grated zest of 1 lemon
Pinch of crushed red pepper flakes or cayenne
1 cup chicken stock, or as needed
1½ tablespoons Dijon mustard
Juice of ½ lemon

Combine all the ingredients and set aside.

ROAST THE CHICKEN

Dry the bird, heat the oven, and roast the chicken as directed on page 26.

CONTINUED

PUT IT ALL TOGETHER

Roast Chicken

Sauce ingredients

Chicken stock or water if needed

Soft Leeks (page 182; optional but earnestly recommended)

Croutons

1/3 cup mixed fresh mint and flat-leaf parsley leaves

After the chicken comes out of the oven, remove it to a platter and set side.

Drain off some of the excess oil from the pan, then add the sauce ingredients. Cook over medium heat for 3 to 4 minutes, whisking to dissolve the mustard. When the sauce has the thickness of heavy cream, check for intense deliciousness. If you think it's too thick, loosen with more stock or water. Remove from the heat.

Cut the chicken into manageable pieces. Add the leeks, if using, to the sauce, then spread the sauce (and leeks) on a platter. Top with the chicken and scatter the croutons and herbs over everything.

CHICKEN *with* AROMATIC HERB-*and*-ALMOND SALAD

In the summertime, room-temperature chicken is fine with me, indeed preferable, and I love to eat it with a fresh salad. There are thousands of ways to go with chicken and salad, and your local farm stand and favorite herbs, spices, and vegetables can be your guide. This salad has its roots in chermoula, a North African mixture that features roughly chopped herbs. Dara Tesser, a wonderful chef and friend who has worked with me for years, came up with it on a warm May afternoon, and it was so good we ended up serving it for the better part of the summer.

SERVES 4

PREP THE CHICKEN

1 organic chicken (2 ½ to 3 pounds), deboned or butterflied (see basic recipe, page 26)
2 to 3 teaspoons kosher salt

Salt the chicken and refrigerate it as directed on page 26.

MEANWHILE, MAKE THE HERB-AND-ALMOND SALAD

½ cup fresh cilantro leaves, roughly chopped
½ cup fresh flat-leaf parsley leaves, roughly chopped
2 tablespoons capers, roughly chopped
¼ cup almond slivers, toasted (page 17)
Grated zest of 1 lemon
1 ½ teaspoons ground cumin
½ teaspoon ground black pepper
½ teaspoon cayenne pepper
2 tablespoons fresh lemon juice
½ teaspoon kosher salt

Combine all the ingredients in a large bowl and set aside.

MAKE THE DRESSING

⅓ cup Greek-style yogurt or labneh
4 Oil-Poached Garlic cloves (page 20), minced
1 tablespoon olive oil
½ teaspoon kosher salt, or to taste
Juice of ½ lemon

Combine the ingredients in a bowl. Season to taste if necessary and set aside.

ROAST THE CHICKEN

Dry the bird, heat the oven, and roast the chicken as directed on page 26.

PUT IT ALL TOGETHER

Dressing
Roast Chicken
Herb-and-Almond Salad

Smear the dressing on a platter. Cut the chicken into manageable pieces. Place the chicken pieces on the platter and shower with the salad. When you eat this dish, your goal is to get some chicken, salad, and dressing on your fork with each bite.

THE THICKNESS OF YOGURT • Look for Greek yogurt or labneh, its Middle Eastern equivalent. They are thicker than ordinary yogurt. I like to start with thick yogurt and then adjust, because it's a lot easier to make thick yogurt thin than it is to make thin yogurt thick.

ROAST CHICKEN *with* SWEET POTATOES, CASHEW BROWN BUTTER, *and* SHARDS *of* CHEESE

Sweet potatoes and cashews share a certain quality of sweetness. Together with nutty-tasting browned butter, they make for a harmony of flavors and textures that can only be described as downright pleasing. Everything in this dish except the chicken can be made well in advance, so it is an ideal make-ahead option for a Sunday lunch or family dinner.

SERVES 4

PREP THE CHICKEN

1 organic chicken (2 ½ to 3 pounds), deboned or butterflied (see basic recipe, page 26)

2 to 3 teaspoons kosher salt

Salt the chicken and refrigerate it as directed on page 26.

MEANWHILE, COOK THE SWEET POTATOES

1 ¼ pounds sweet potatoes

Preheat the oven to 350°F. Fit the sweet potatoes snugly into an ovenproof pot and cover tightly with foil and then a lid. Roast until very soft, 1 hour and 15 minutes to 1 hour and 45 minutes. (The sweet potatoes can be cooked ahead and refrigerated for up to 24 hours.)

COOK THE CASHEWS AND ROSEMARY

½ cup cashews

1 sprig of fresh rosemary

4 tablespoons (½ stick) unsalted butter

¼ teaspoon kosher salt

Chop the cashews into smallish pieces. Strip the leaves off the rosemary sprig and chop them. Set a sieve over a small heatproof bowl.

Heat the butter in a small saucepan over medium heat. Add the cashews and cook, stirring with a heatproof spatula, until the butter has mostly stopped foaming and has browned. Pour the cashews and butter into the sieve and then return the butter to the saucepan. Add the rosemary and cook over medium heat until the foaming dies down, then cook for another 30 seconds and pour over the cashews in the sieve. Transfer the cashews to a plate, salt them, and reserve the butter.

MAKE THE BROWN BUTTER VINAIGRETTE

Brown butter (from above)

2 tablespoons white wine vinegar or white balsamic vinegar

¼ teaspoon kosher salt

Combine the butter with the vinegar and salt.

ROAST THE CHICKEN

Dry the bird, heat the oven, and roast the chicken as directed on page 26.

PUT IT ALL TOGETHER

4 ounces aged sheep's-milk cheese, such as Manchego

Brown Butter Vinaigrette

Sweet potatoes

Roast Chicken

Cashews and rosemary

Slice the cheese into thinnish slices; don't worry if it crumbles. Rewarm the vinaigrette in a small pan. Reheat the sweet potatoes if necessary.

Cut the chicken and sweet potatoes into manageable pieces and place on a platter. Scatter the cheese, cashews, and rosemary all over and spoon the hot vinaigrette over everything.

CHICKEN *with* GRILLED ZUCCHINI *and* PUMPKIN SEED TAHINI

It's July and hot as a blacksmith's forge. You want roast chicken, but the thought of the oven going full blast is not alluring. But if you have a covered grill, you can prep the tahini in the kitchen and then cook the chicken and zucchini outside. You'll have leftover pumpkin seed tahini, which is heaven with crudités, or use it instead of peanut butter for a beguiling version of a PB & J sandwich.

SERVES 4

PREP THE CHICKEN

1 organic chicken (2½ to 3 pounds), deboned or butterflied (see headnote, page 26)
2 to 3 teaspoons kosher salt

Salt the chicken and refrigerate it as directed on page 26.

MEANWHILE, MAKE THE PUMPKIN SEED TAHINI

½ cup pumpkin seeds, toasted (page 17)
3 tablespoons water, or as needed
1 tablespoon Dukkah (page 39)
½ teaspoon kosher salt
1 to 2 tablespoons olive oil, as needed

Put the seeds, water, spice, and salt in a blender or food processor and blend to a smooth paste. You want the mixture to spin easily, so you may need to add another tablespoon or two of water. Add the olive oil and blend again. Set aside.

GRILL THE ZUCCHINI

2 or 3 medium zucchini or yellow summer squash, or a combination

Prepare a medium fire in a grill.

Cut the squash lengthwise into ½-inch-thick slabs. Grill for 3 to 5 five minutes per side, until softened but with some bite; you want some grill marks. Not black, though. Remove and let cool.

You'll need a medium-hot fire to cook the chicken.

PREP THE HERB MIX

¾ cup fresh flat-leaf parsley leaves, chopped
¼ cup fresh tarragon leaves, chopped
¼ cup olive oil
Juice of 1 lemon
Cayenne or Aleppo pepper to taste (optional)
½ to 1 teaspoon kosher salt (to taste)

Combine the ingredients in a bowl.

Chop the zucchini into bite-sized pieces and add to the bowl with the herbs.

COOK THE CHICKEN

Set the skillet on the grill grate and slick with oil. Put in the chicken skin side down and cook, with the grill open, until you have some color on the skin, 2 to 5 minutes. Close the grill and continue cooking until the chicken is done, 10 to 20 minutes, depending on whether the chicken was deboned or butterflied. The temperature of the thickest part of the thigh should read 155°F to 160°F.

PUT IT ALL TOGETHER

Chicken
Pumpkin Seed Tahini
Zucchini and herbs
½ lemon (optional)

Cut the chicken into manageable pieces. Smear the tahini on a platter and place the chicken and the zucchini and herb salad on top. Squeeze some lemon over the whole thing if you like.

BROWN-
BUTTER
HANGER
STEAK

BROWN-BUTTER HANGER STEAK

BASIC RECIPE

I've cooked thousands of hanger steaks, an economical, flavorful cut, and I've come to an unusual conclusion: *Char can be overrated.* Indeed, it's an impediment to the cooking of a perfect juicy hanger steak. Hanger tastes better barely seared at all and cooked just to medium-rare. Finish it with brown butter, and you'll get all the "charred" flavor you need. And you will be happy to find that my method results in a smoke-free kitchen and you'll get a tender, beefy steak that is rosy pink from edge to edge.

There's a thick sinewy membrane that runs lengthwise down the steak that must be removed before cooking. In all likelihood, a butcher will have done this for you, but it's not hard to do on your own.

SERVES 4

One 1½- to 2-pound hanger steak
About 1 teaspoon kosher salt
Canola or grapeseed oil to film the pan
2 to 3 tablespoons unsalted butter
2 garlic cloves, smashed, left unpeeled (optional)
A few sprigs of fresh rosemary and/or thyme (optional)

Preheat the oven to 400°F, with a rack in the lower third. Place a rack on a baking sheet for cooking the steak.

Portion the steaks: For a typical adult, 6 ounces is a small steak and 8 is a large one. Salt the steak a little more than you feel comfortable doing.

Film a large skillet with oil and heat over medium-high heat until the oil just starts to shimmer. Gently lay in the steaks. Cook for 1 to 2 minutes on each side, until grayish with faint blushes of mahogany. Forget everything anyone ever told you about getting a good sear: This is just a little heat massage that lets the meat know it's going to be cooked. If there's a little uncooked pink here and there, don't sweat it.

Transfer the steak to the rack on the baking sheet and put it in the lower third of the oven. Pour the fat out of the skillet and add the butter and the garlic and herbs if using (see Note); set aside. If the steak is 1½ inches thick, it'll probably take about 12 minutes to reach rare at the thickest part. Flip the steaks once or twice during the time they are in the oven. To check the temperature, insert an instant-read thermometer at a 30-degree angle (the steak is so thin that it's hard to get an accurate reading if you push the thermometer straight down); pull the steaks from the oven at an internal temperature of 120°F. Let rest, uncovered, on the rack for 10 minutes; the steaks will continue cooking to medium-rare in the residual heat.

Finish the steaks in the brown butter: Heat the skillet over medium-high heat. As it warms, the butter will foam and, as you swirl it around, it will turn caramel brown. Add the steaks and bathe them in the fragrant butter. You can use a spoon to baste, or do as I do and use a pair tongs to turn the steaks over again and again, anointing the meat with the butter as it rewarms. After about 90 seconds, the steaks will be beautifully brown and ready to serve.

Slice the steaks on the bias, across the grain, and arrange the slices on a platter so that you can see the red/pink interior. Spoon the brown butter over the steak.

Note: *You can serve the steak as is or, to add a bit more flavor, add 2 smashed unpeeled garlic cloves and a few sprigs of fresh rosemary or thyme to the skillet when you add the butter (right after you cook the steaks on the stovetop at the beginning of the recipe).*

HANGER STEAK *with* CRISPY DUKKAH POTATOES

Steak and potatoes are so enshrined in our food culture that they surely need no further selling from me. But the addition of dukkah spice to this hallowed combination brings its own new pleasure. Dukkah is a catch-all name for an Egyptian combination of aromatic spices and nuts that I use on roasts, sautéed vegetables, and fish. I make up batches and always have some on hand. I'm pretty agnostic as to what nut to use: almonds, hazelnuts, pistachio—whatever is on hand and catches my fancy that day.

SERVES 4

MAKE THE DUKKAH

2 tablespoons coriander seeds
1 tablespoon cumin seeds
¼ cup sesame seeds
¼ cup nuts (pistachios, almonds, peanuts, hazelnuts, almonds . . . all are fair game)

Preheat the oven to 400°F.

Spread the coriander seeds, cumin seeds, sesame seeds, and nuts on a small baking sheet or combine in a skillet and toast in the oven for 10 minutes. Rotate the pan and cook for another 5 minutes, or until thoroughly toasted. (A little overcooked is better than a little undercooked; a touch of burn here and there is preferable and in the spirit of dukkah.) Remove from the oven and let cool to room temperature. Leave the oven on.

Grind the seeds and nuts using whatever grinding tool you prefer—a mortar and pestle, a spice grinder, or a blender—leaving them somewhat coarse. Don't overprocess, or the nuts and seeds can get a little gummy. (You will only need a generous tablespoon of the dukkah for the potatoes; freeze leftovers.)

COOK THE CRISPY DUKKAH POTATOES

8 medium Yukon Gold potatoes (about 2 pounds), peeled
Kosher salt
Canola or grapeseed oil (enough to fill the pan ¼ inch deep)
2 tablespoons unsalted butter
1 heaping tablespoon Dukkah

Put the potatoes in a saucepan filled with enough cold water to cover them and bring to a boil over medium-high heat. When they are soft, about 10 minutes after the water boils, drain them and smash on a cutting board to break them apart into bite-sized chunks; season well with salt.

Heat the oil in a large ovenproof skillet over medium-high heat. Add the potatoes and fry for 2 minutes, turning them once or twice. Transfer the skillet to the oven and roast for 10 minutes; remove the pan from the oven and set aside; toss the potatoes after 4 minutes. Leave the oven on.

CONTINUED

MAKE THE BROWN-BUTTER HANGER STEAK

Portion and salt the steak as directed on page 38. Cook it on the stovetop, and then in the oven, and finish in the brown butter as directed.

MEANWHILE, FINISH THE CRISPY DUKKAH POTATOES

Place the skillet back over medium heat. (Remember the skillet handle is *hot* from the oven.) Add the butter and toss to coat the potatoes as the butter melts. Remove the crisped potatoes to a bowl with a slotted spoon and toss with the tablespoon dukkah and a pinch of salt.

PUT IT ALL TOGETHER

Brown-Butter Hanger Steak
Crispy Dukkah Potatoes

Slice the steak against the grain and overlap the slices on a platter. Spoon the pan juices over the slices and place the potatoes alongside.

"Jean-Michel!... Your cholesterol!!!"

HANGER STEAK *with* COMPOUND BUTTERS

If you've never had a beautiful piece of steak with a dab of compound butter smeared over it, I am happy here to offer you a true culinary treasure—actually, five of them. There is no end to the herbs and spices, along with dried mushrooms, garlic, shallots, chives, and/or ramps, that you can use to make compound butters. They deliver much of the fun and flavor of labor-intensive sauces with much less work. You can melt compound butter on steaks or roasted vegetables, make an amazing (as in amazingly simple) crostino, cook it into your scrambled eggs, melt some into a baked potato. Bottom line, double the recipes . . . or even triple them.

All of these recipes call for softened butter. You can leave it at room temperature for 20 minutes to an hour, or soften it in the microwave. The method is the same for all of the butters. First prep the herbs—even if you are using a food processor, you still need to mince the herbs beforehand to achieve a nice uniformly green butter. Next, combine the herbs and other ingredients except the butter in a bowl and mix with a whisk or spoon, or a rubber spatula. Add the softened butter and work it over with a wooden spoon until everything is combined. Alternatively, pulse all the ingredients a few times in a food processor until the butter is a uniform color. You may have to scrape the sides down a few times with a spatula.

All of these recipes make a little more than ½ cup. You can store the butter in the fridge for up to 5 days or in the freezer for 6 months.

FINISHING HANGER STEAK WITH A COMPOUND BUTTER

Portion and cook the steaks as directed on page 38. Finish the steaks with the brown butter as directed, then slice, put on a platter, and dab the compound butter on the slices. You can put the platter in the warm oven for 30 to 60 seconds to partially melt the compound butter.

CONTINUED

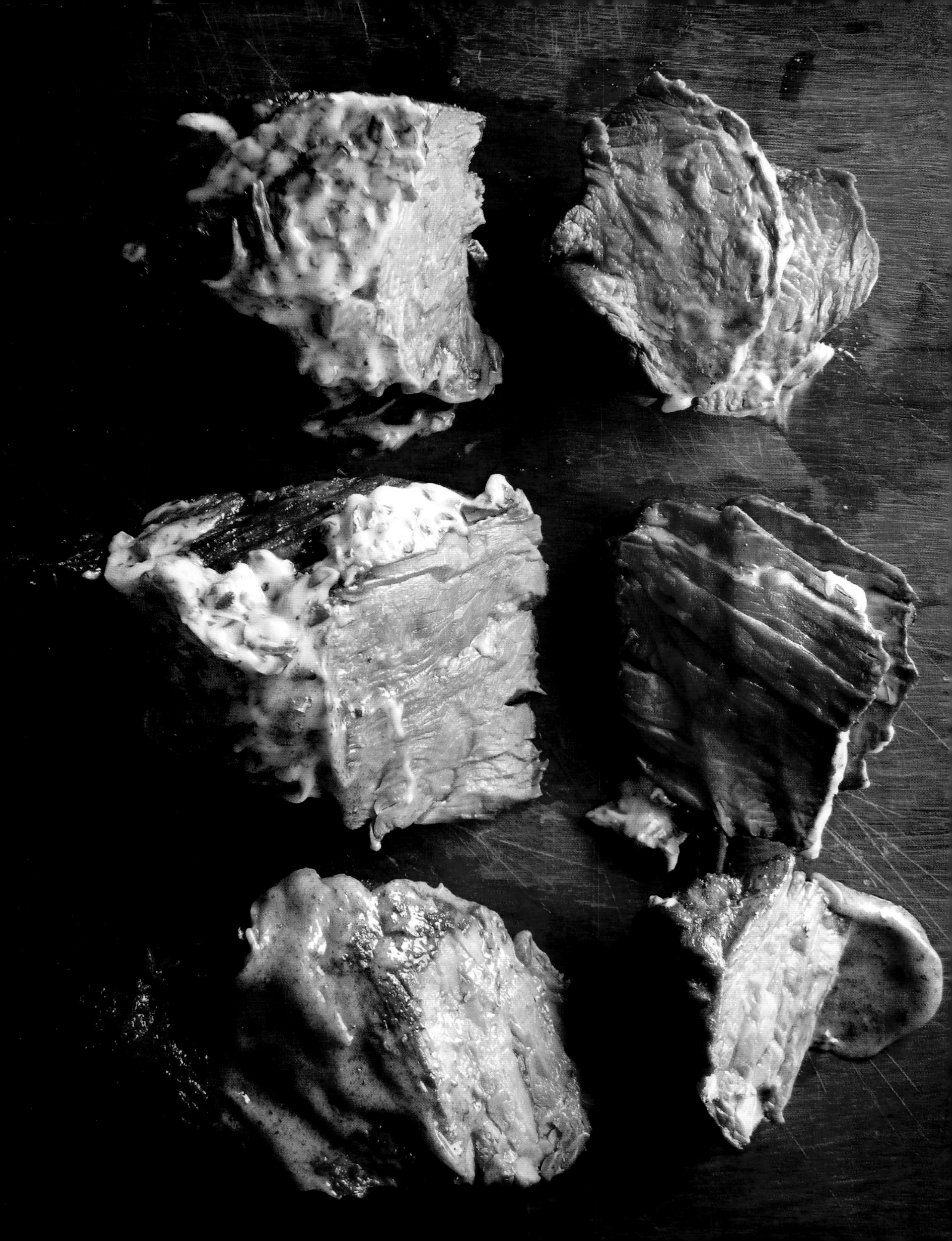

Ramp Leaf Butter

Ramps mark the blessed return of the color green each spring. They pop up when the fiddlehead ferns and morels appear in the bottomland and the trout and shad are there for your hook and line in the rivers. We make pounds and pounds of ramp butter for the restaurant because I think its flavor and emerald sheen are spectacular. You can use it with sautéed or grilled vegetables or poached fillets of white-fleshed fish, especially boned shad. The butter will keep in the freezer for months, so it's a fine way to stretch the fleeting ramp season.

1/4 to 1/3 cup minced ramp leaves (reserve the stems for another use, such as pickling them)

1/2 teaspoon kosher salt

8 tablespoons (1 stick) unsalted butter, softened

Put the ramps and salt in a medium bowl or a food processor. Add the butter and mix thoroughly. Transfer to a container with a tight-fitting lid and refrigerate. Remove from the refrigerator 15 minutes before serving.

Cilantro-Cumin Butter with Red Pepper and Lime Zest

Great with steaks and also quite nice with pork, roasted carrots, and grilled chicken and in (or on) scrambled eggs, but don't let me stop you there. If it seems good in your imagination, it will probably be good on your palate.

1/4 cup fresh cilantro leaves, minced

1/2 teaspoon ground cumin

1/2 teaspoon crushed red pepper flakes

1/2 teaspoon kosher salt, or more if desired

Grated zest of 1 lime

8 tablespoons (1 stick) unsalted butter, softened

Put the cilantro, cumin, red pepper flakes, salt, and lime zest in a medium bowl or a food processor. Add the butter and mix thoroughly. Transfer to a container with a tight-fitting lid and refrigerate. Remove from the refrigerator 15 minutes before serving.

Rosemary, Thyme, and Poached-Garlic Anisette Butter

This butter is also terrific on pork chops, roast chicken, and roasted mushrooms. Any anise-flavored liqueur works fine; you can omit the liqueur entirely if you prefer.

Note: *You can mince both herbs at the same time, rather than doing them one by one. Less of a chore that way.*

2 to 4 Oil-Poached Garlic cloves (page 20), mashed

2 tablespoons minced mixed fresh thyme and rosemary

3/4 teaspoon kosher salt

1 teaspoon pastis, Ricard, sambuca, or anisette

8 tablespoons (1 stick) unsalted butter, softened

Combine the garlic, herbs, salt, and liqueur in a medium bowl or a food processor. Add the butter and mix thoroughly. Transfer to a container with a tight-fitting lid and refrigerate. Remove from the refrigerator 15 minutes before serving.

CONTINUED

Ground Porcini, Brown Sugar, and Sage Butter

There's something about the combination of this porcini butter and the brown butter the steak cooks in that makes the meat taste like well-aged beef. This butter is great on sweet potatoes as well, and it's also nice on autumn squash and yams.

2 tablespoons ground dried porcini (you can grind the mushrooms yourself or buy porcini power)

1 tablespoon light brown sugar

1 teaspoon chopped fresh sage

½ teaspoon kosher salt

8 tablespoons (1 stick) unsalted butter, softened

Put the porcini, sugar, sage, and salt in a medium bowl or a food processor. Add the butter and mix thoroughly. Transfer to a container with a tight-fitting lid and refrigerate. Remove from the refrigerator 15 minutes before serving.

Tarragon-Shallot Butter

This butter has the flavors of classic Béarnaise sauce, but with fewer ingredients, no eggs, and less fuss.

¼ brimming cup fresh flat-leaf parsley or chervil leaves, minced

2 tablespoons chopped fresh tarragon

1 to 2 tablespoons minced Oil-Poached Shallots (page 20)

½ teaspoon kosher salt

Grated zest of ½ lemon

8 tablespoons (1 stick) unsalted butter, softened

Combine the parsley, tarragon, shallots, salt, and lemon zest in a medium bowl or a food processor. Add the butter and mix thoroughly. Transfer to a container with a tight-fitting lid and refrigerate. Remove from the refrigerator 15 minutes before serving.

STEAK *and* EGGS

I like to get up early. I guess I'm more of a fisherman than a chef in that regard. Later, once I'm off the water, steak and eggs with asparagus and spring onions are a springtime weekend favorite, a robust midmorning meal that fortifies us for a Saturday beach walk or a city hike.

The sauce is a relative of one we used when I worked at Prune and is as versatile as any you'll find. Don't hesitate to double the recipe and sock some of it away in the freezer for a rainy day.

SERVES 4

PREPARE THE SPRING ONIONS

1 bunch (3 or 4) spring onions

Trim the root ends of the onions and, if you think they need it, the tops as well. Blanch them in boiling water for 7 minutes, or until they are soft to the tooth.

MAKE THE 6-MINUTE EGGS

4 large eggs

Boil the eggs for 6 minutes as directed on page 241. Peel. Leave the water in the pot for rewarming the eggs later.

MAKE THE SAUCE

Brown Butter made from 4 tablespoons (½ stick) unsalted butter (page 22)
About ⅛ teaspoon cayenne pepper
1 heaping teaspoon Dijon mustard
1 tablespoon red wine vinegar

Transfer the brown butter to a small bowl or ramekin and add the cayenne. Cool it in an ice bath or in the fridge for a few minutes, until it is the texture of Crisco. Whisk in the mustard, followed by the red wine vinegar. Set aside.

MAKE THE BROWN-BUTTER HANGER STEAK

Portion and salt the steak as directed on page 38. Cook it on the stovetop, and then in the oven. Set aside to rest.

MEANWHILE, MAKE THE ASPARAGUS AND ONIONS

Canola or grapeseed oil to film the skillet
Blanched spring onions (from above)
½ bunch (about 8 ounces) asparagus, stalks trimmed
1 tablespoon chopped fresh tarragon
1 tablespoon chopped fresh flat-leaf parsley
Squeeze of lemon
Kosher salt

Film a large skillet with oil and set over medium-high heat. Sauté the onions and asparagus for 4 to 8 minutes, depending on thickness of the asparagus, until cooked to your liking: Asparagus is like fried eggs—everybody has their own particular bliss point. Toss with the herbs, lemon juice, and salt to taste.

PUT IT ALL TOGETHER

Brown-Butter Hanger Steak
6-Minute Eggs
Asparagus and onions
Sauce

Finish the steak in the brown butter as directed on page 38. Rewarm the eggs in the hot water.

Lay the asparagus and onions on a platter. Slice the steak against the grain and lay it on top of the asparagus and onions. One at a time, pinch into the white of each egg and gently pull it apart—the yolks should be a bit runny—and add to the platter. Spoon the sauce over everything. Serve.

STEAK *with* TOMATO SALAD *and* AROMATIC SPICES

This spice mix is derived from a Syrian blend that is traditionally made with the famous Aleppo pepper. Providentially, the pepper is now found in many places other than that tragically war-torn city. Aleppo pepper is a bit gentler than standard crushed red pepper flakes, but still adds a bit of spicy heat. The spice mix also includes sumac—dried red flakes of dried sumac berries—which adds tartness like lemon juice but without liquid. The pepper and sumac combine with the warm aromatic spices for a sense of the exotic. If you don't have all of these ingredients on hand, go with what you have in the assurance that some grandmother, somewhere in the Middle East, has done the same and the family still enjoyed it.

SERVES 4

MAKE THE BROWN-BUTTER HANGER STEAK

Portion and salt the steak as directed on page 38. Cook the steak on the stovetop and then in the oven. Set aside to rest.

MEANWHILE, MAKE THE SPICE MIX

¼ teaspoon ground coriander
¼ teaspoon ground black pepper
¼ teaspoon ground allspice
1 teaspoon ground sumac (available at specialty markets and online)
1 teaspoon Aleppo pepper, ½ teaspoon crushed red pepper flakes, or a dash of cayenne pepper
Kosher salt to taste

Combine all the ingredients in a bowl and mix well.

MAKE THE TOMATO SALAD

Spice Mix
4 fresh oregano or mint leaves (if the mint leaves are huge, tear them up)
2 tablespoons olive oil
1 garlic clove, grated or minced and mashed to a puree with a little salt (page 70)
1 to 2 tablespoons fresh lemon juice
1 tablespoon kosher salt
¾ pound cherry tomatoes, preferably mixed colors, halved or quartered

Combine the spice mix, oregano or mint, olive oil, garlic, lemon juice, and salt. Put the tomatoes in a bowl, pour over the dressing, and toss. Set aside.

MAKE THE YOGURT DRESSING

1 cup Greek-style yogurt or labneh
1 garlic clove, grated or minced
Kosher salt

Put the yogurt or labneh and garlic in a small bowl and whisk until the mixture is smooth. Season with salt.

PUT IT ALL TOGETHER

Brown-Butter Hanger Steak
Yogurt Dressing
Tomato Salad

Finish the steak in the brown butter as directed on page 38. Slice the steak against the grain. Make a bold smear of the dressing on a platter. Pile on the steak and the tomato salad. Dribble any remaining liquid from the tomato salad all over the place.

HANGER TARTARE

Hanger steak delivers a pungent wild-game flavor and springy texture that distinguishes it from the milder filet mignon traditionally used in beef tartare. Dried dulse, a seaweed that is now relatively common, has a way of boosting savory flavors.

SERVES 4

PREP THE HANGER STEAK

One 10-ounce hanger steak

Get out your sharpest knife and trim the steak of any fat and sinew as best you can, then cut it into ⅛- to ¼-inch dice. Don't worry about making perfect squares. Cover and refrigerate.

MAKE THE EGG YOLK SAUCE

3 large egg yolks
2 teaspoons Worcestershire sauce

Beat the egg yolks with a fork in a small bowl to break them up. Whisk in the Worcestershire. Set aside.

MAKE THE TOASTED SUNFLOWER SPICE MIX

2 tablespoons sunflower seeds, toasted (page 17)
1 teaspoon dried dulse flakes
1 teaspoon Aleppo pepper or ½ teaspoon crushed red pepper flakes
1 teaspoon flaky sea salt

Grind the sunflower seeds and dulse in a spice grinder; it doesn't have to be powdery smooth. Combine all of the ingredients and set aside.

PUT IT ALL TOGETHER

Chopped hanger steak
Toasted Sunflower Spice Mix
2 tablespoons minced fresh flat-leaf parsley
1 tablespoon minced fresh tarragon
¼ cup olive oil
Egg Yolk Sauce
Kosher salt

Combine the steak, sunflower seed mix, parsley, tarragon, and 2 tablespoons of the olive oil in a bowl and mix thoroughly. Taste and adjust the seasoning. Spread the tartare out on a plate and drizzle the egg yolk sauce and the remaining 2 tablespoons olive oil over it. Serve immediately.

Pork-Shoulder Pot Roast

PORK-SHOULDER POT ROAST

BASIC RECIPE

When I want essence of pork, pure pork and nothing else, I turn to a pot-roasting technique that I learned in my early days in a restaurant kitchen. The result is juicy and uncompromisingly porky. I start by salting the meat a day or three in advance. Then, when it's time to cook, double-sealing the pot—once with aluminum foil and then with the lid—ensures that the salted meat releases and the pot retains a wonderful ambrosial liquid as it cooks. This liquid is a gift to the cook: It benefits almost any recipe. Guard that juice as you would a family heirloom.

Note: *I have given the amount of salt in teaspoons. But if you, as I do, want to be more precise, a 4-pound butt, for example, weighs 1,814 grams. If you salt it at between 1.1 percent and 1.5 percent of its weight, that would be between 20 and 25 grams of salt, or roughly 2 to 2½ tablespoons, for the 4-pound roast.*

MAKES ENOUGH PORK FOR SEVERAL MEALS; *refer to the recipes that follow*

SALT THE PORK (1 OR 2 DAYS AHEAD)

1 boneless pork shoulder roast (Boston butt; 4 to 6 pounds)
2 to 2½ tablespoons kosher salt for a 4-pound butt to 3½ to 4 tablespoons salt for a 6-pound butt

Put the meat in a large bowl and shower it with the salt on all sides, rubbing it in with your hands. Your goal is for all of the salt to adhere to the meat.

Put the meat in a large Ziploc bag or cover the bowl with plastic wrap and refrigerate for 12 to 48 hours. I like to leave it for 1 to 3 days so that the salt really permeates the meat.

COOK THE PORK

Preheat the oven to 275°F, with a rack in the middle.

Place the pork in a Dutch oven. Seal the Dutch oven with aluminum foil and then secure the foil with the lid. Set the pot in the oven. At this low temperature, the roast will take about 3 hours to reach 180°F to 190°F, which is the magic point when the pork shoulder is perfectly done.

I find it's best to cook the pork the day before serving it. Make sure to reserve the *jus*—liquid released during the cooking—it's gold. So is the fat. You'll need them for the following recipes. Refrigerate the pork and liquid separately. Once the liquid is chilled, you can skim off the solidified fat to use in any recipe that calls for pork fat.

Love is Love

TORN PORK *with* CLAMS *and* HERBS

I once read an essay by a combat journalist who recounted a World War II meal he'd had in Italy. Having been perilously close to the front lines, he was pulled back to a cozy inn and, it being Italy, food ensued: a dish of roast pork and clams. Even though it's typical in many cuisines for pork sausage to rub elbows with clams, the thought of surrounding a pork roast with steamed clams really blew my mind. I gave it a shot and discovered that the heady funkiness of pork marries very congenially with clams. Why, you ask, is the pork torn, rather than sliced, cubed, or pulled? I find that attacking it this way results in chunks that offer fissures and crevasses, hills and valleys to bathe in the delicious *jus* left from the pot-roasting. It's the same logic as forking open an English muffin to create spaces for butter to fill.

SERVES 4

Preheat the oven to 400°F for rewarming the pork.

TEAR THE PORK

1 ½ pounds Pork-Shoulder Pot Roast (page 52)

Tear the pork into four 2- to 3-inch hunks.

COOK THE CLAMS

2 cups white wine
3 tablespoons minced Oil-Poached Garlic (page 20)
¼ teaspoon crushed red pepper flakes
24 littleneck clams

Combine the wine, garlic, and red pepper flakes in a Dutch oven (or other pot big enough to hold most of the clams in a single layer), bring to a boil over high heat, and cook until the alcohol has burned off, about 5 minutes. Add the clams and pork jus, reduce the heat to medium, cover, and cook for 4 to 5 minutes. When the clams are open—or at least smiling—you're good. Don't worry if they all haven't opened completely. I pay no attention to the old adage that if a clam doesn't open, it's gone bad—that's just a superstition. Just as some safes take longer to crack than others, so do some clams.

MEANWHILE, REWARM THE PORK

Place the torn pork on a baking sheet, slide into the oven, and cook for about 10 minutes, so the pork gets some crispy edges.

PUT IT ALL TOGETHER

Torn pork
Clams with their liquid
¼ cup fresh oregano leaves
⅓ cup fresh mint leaves (if they are big, tear them in half)

Divide the pork among four wide shallow bowls. Add the clams, scatter on the herbs, and spoon the liquid over it all. Crusty bread alongside, toasted and rubbed with garlic, wouldn't be half bad.

TORN PORK *with* PISTACHIO-GINGER SAUCE

If I were given my own desert island—one with a gentle climate, fertile land, and just the right amount of rain—I would raise spices from India, Vietnam, and Jamaica, along with pistachios, chilies, and pigs. Here I combine a lot of spices in a dish whose launching point was a South Asian green curry.

Note: *I peel ginger simply by cutting off the skin with a paring knife, but you can use a peeler. Rather than discarding the trimmings, I often add them to the water for cooking rice, then discard it before serving. It's subtle but sublime. If you feel like cooking up some rice this way, it will put a ribbon and a bow on this dish.*

SERVES 4

MAKE THE CURRY SPICE MIX

1 teaspoon ground turmeric
½ teaspoon ground cumin
½ teaspoon ground fenugreek
¼ teaspoon ground nutmeg
¼ teaspoon ground cinnamon

Mix all the spices together; set aside.

MAKE THE PISTACHIO-GINGER SAUCE

2 medium leeks
3 tablespoons oil from Oil-Poached Garlic and Shallots (page 20) or olive oil
1 jalapeño, minced, with seeds or not, depending on your personal heat quotient
3 garlic cloves, minced
2 tablespoons minced peeled ginger (trimmings reserved for cooking rice, if you like; see headnote)
Curry Spice Mix
⅓ cup finely ground pistachios
⅓ brimming cup fresh cilantro leaves, chopped
½ cup reserved pork jus from the pot roast
1 (12-ounce) can unsweetened coconut milk (1 ½ cups)
Grated zest and juice of 1 lime

Trim away the tops of the leeks and discard or set aside for another use. Halve each leek lengthwise, then rinse under cold water, making sure to rid them of any grit and sand. Slice each half crosswise into thin half-moons.

Put the leeks in a large saucepan, along with the oil and jalapeño, and cook over medium-low heat for 2 to 3 minutes. Add the garlic and ginger and cook for another minute. Add the spice mix and stir until fragrant. Add the pistachios, cilantro, pork jus, and coconut milk and cook for 20 minutes to fully marry the flavors. Stir in the lime zest and juice (save a splash of lime for a finishing touch). Set aside.

MEANWHILE, TEAR THE PORK

1 ½ pounds Pork-Shoulder Pot Roast (page 52)

Tear the pork into four 2- to 3-inch hunks.

Preheat the oven to 400°F.

WARM AND CRISP THE PORK

¼ cup reserved pork fat (from the pork roast), or oil from Oil-Poached Garlic or Shallots (page 20) or canola or grapeseed oil

Torn pork

¼ cup reserved pork jus

Heat the pork fat or oil in a large skillet over medium-high heat. Add the torn pork and sear; it's okay to crowd the pork pieces in the pan. The fat should bubble nicely all around the pork. When you've got color on a couple sides of the pork, no more than 5 minutes, pour off the fat—or, if you like the fat as much as I do, don't pour it off.

Transfer the pork (and fat, if you like) to a baking pan, add the reserved jus, and finish warming the pork in the oven, 5 to 10 minutes.

PUT IT ALL TOGETHER

Torn pork

Pistachio-Ginger Sauce

Chopped fresh cilantro for garnish

Put the pork in a large serving bowl, pour the sauce over, and garnish with cilantro and a splash of lime juice.

SLICED PORK SHOULDER *with* WILTED GREENS, ROASTED TOMATOES, *and* CROUTONS

While it's true that nothing beats a sweet summer tomato, one of the few culinary triumphs of modern agriculture is good cherry tomatoes even when other tomatoes aren't in season. This recipe calls for Swiss chard, but you can substitute kale, broccoli rabe, spigarello, or another green—in other words, pick your green and cook until tender.

SERVES 4

BLANCH THE CHARD

1 bunch Swiss chard, tough center ribs removed

Bring a large pot of water to a rolling boil. Drop in the greens. After 3 minutes, pull a leaf out and taste it. The cooking will "carry over" a little, so you want to remove the chard just before it's tender.

Meanwhile, set a rack on a baking sheet and cover it with parchment paper or a dish towel. When the chard is cooked, drain it and lay the leaves out on the covered rack to drain.

COOK THE TOMATOES

2 tablespoons oil from Oil-Poached Garlic or Shallots (page 20) or olive oil

1 pint mixed colors or red cherry tomatoes, rinsed and any stems removed

3 garlic cloves, roughly chopped

Kosher salt

1 tablespoon white wine vinegar

Slick a large heavy-bottomed skillet with the olive oil and set it over high heat. When you see a wisp of smoke, add the tomatoes, garlic, and a sprinkling of salt and cook, keeping the tomatoes moving, either with a spoon or by shaking the pan, for about 90 seconds, until they wilt a little and their skins begin to wrinkle and crack. Add the white wine vinegar and reduce for 30 seconds. Remove to a bowl and set aside.

MAKE THE CROUTONS

1 slice whole wheat bread (about 1 inch thick)

2 to 3 tablespoons oil from Oil-Poached Garlic or Shallots (page 20) or olive oil

Kosher salt

1/8 teaspoon cayenne pepper

Grated zest of 1 lemon

Leaves from 2 sprigs of fresh thyme

Pull the bread apart with your fingers; the pieces should be just a little smaller than chocolate chips.

Add the oil to a skillet set over medium-high heat, then add the bread and cook, stirring, until the croutons are mahogany in color, 3 to 5 minutes; manage the temperature so the oil never smokes. Pour the croutons and oil into a strainer set over a bowl, then spread the croutons out on a paper towel to drain briefly.

Transfer the croutons to a bowl and toss with salt to taste, the cayenne, lemon zest, and thyme, using your hands. Lick your fingers.

PUT IT ALL TOGETHER

8 to 16 (¼- to ½-inch-thick) slices Pork-Shoulder Pot Roast (page 52; the pork should be cold for optional slicing; allow 2 slices per person for small portions, 4 each for larger portions)

¼ cup reserved pork jus from the pot roast

A little of the reserved pork fat

Blanched Swiss chard

Tomatoes

Croutons

A squeeze or two of lemon

Flaky sea salt (optional)

Set a skillet over medium-low heat, add the pork, pork jus, and pork fat, and heat until the pork is warm.

To serve, lay alternating slices of pork and the chard leaves on a platter; messy plating is encouraged. Pour any remaining jus from the pan over the pork and chard. Strew the tomatoes over, then spoon their juices over and shower the platter with croutons as if they have fallen from the sky. Finish with the lemon juice and perhaps some flaky salt, keeping in mind that the pork and jus are already salted from the curing and cooking.

PORK SANDWICHES

A Theory of the Sandwich

As a hiker, chef, traveler, fisherman, carpenter, and TV watcher, I have strong feelings about sandwiches. All sandwiches, of course, depend on the flavor and texture of the ingredients, but of nearly equal importance are design and construction. Remember, your mouth is only so big, and the damn thing has to fit in it. It also has to hold together. The bread-to-filling ratio has to be right. And while you are at, get good bread: It's just as important as what goes between the slices.

A crispy sandwich wants a crust that is both crunchy and brittle. Bread with a brittle crust that snaps as you bite into it is a signal to our genetic memory that something good is about to be eaten. Scientists refer to this tendency of crusts to shatter under pressure as "indentation fractography." You don't want, for example, low indentation fractography in window glass, but in a crusty sandwich, it makes for love at first bite. The equation that scientists use to measure this is $\frac{e}{\sigma Y}\tan(\beta) = 6(1-v)\left(\frac{rZ}{a}\right)^3 - 4(1-2\nu)$, and I have no idea if that is right or even what it means. You can try reading "Indentation techniques for evaluating the fracture toughness of biomaterials and hard tissues" in *Journal of the Mechanical Behavior of Biomedical Materials* by J. J. Kruzic, D. K. Kim, K. J. Koester, and R. O. Ritchie. Or, much easier . . . you can take my word for it.

Then you need to consider how you lubricate the sandwich—whether you use mayo, butter, mustard, olive oil, tapenade, or schmaltz (chicken fat)—so that each mouthful slips effortlessly down your gullet. This is also an opportunity to add some supporting or contrasting flavors.

The pork sandwiches that follow were inspired by what I had on hand at the time. That's the only way I know how to make sandwiches. The best recipes are born where appetite meets the larder. Feel free to make up your own variations.

PORK SANDWICHES *with* CRUNCHY PISTACHIO SPREAD

One Christmas, when I was in Venice with my family, we fell in love with the *cicchetti* (snacks) served in many bars. One of the more surprising choices was a crostino with chunky pistachio spread. The memory of this while drifting off to sleep one night gave birth to this sandwich.

Note: *You'll have more pistachio spread than you need for 4 sandwiches. It makes a great crostini topping.*

SERVES 4 *(you could make 8 or 10 sandwiches from the whole pork roast)*

MAKE THE PISTACHIO SPREAD

⅔ cup unsalted pistachios

2 tablespoons water

1 or 2 tablespoons oil from Oil-Poached Garlic or Shallots (page 20) or olive oil

½ teaspoon kosher salt, or to taste

A few drizzles of reserved pork jus from the pot roast if needed

Combine the pistachios, water, oil, and salt in a blender or food processor and run until the nuts are pretty broken up—enough that the mixture will be spreadable, but still with some crunch. If the mixture needs to be thinned out for optimal spreadability, add a little pork jus. Check the seasoning for salt. Set aside.

WARM THE BREAD

1 baguette or other long loaf

Preheat the oven to 350°F.

Cut the bread into sandwich-sized lengths. Put on a baking sheet and warm in the oven for 5 to 7 minutes.

MEANWHILE, WARM THE PORK

12 (¼- to ½-inch-thick) slices Pork-Shoulder Pot Roast (page 52; the pork should be cold for optimal slicing)

¼ cup reserved pork jus from the pot roast

2 medium garlic cloves, minced

1 teaspoon crushed red pepper flakes

Put the pork in a large skillet, add the jus, garlic, and crushed red pepper flakes, and gently warm over a medium flame on the stovetop. Keep your eye on it.

PUT IT ALL TOGETHER

Warmed bread

½ cup Pistachio Spread

Warmed pork

8 to 12 anchovy fillets (your call)

1 cup fresh mint leaves

½ lemon

1 tablespoon plus 1 teaspoon oil from Oil-Poached Garlic or Shallots (page 20) or olive oil

4 Oil-Poached Garlic cloves (page 20), mashed (optional)

Split the bread and slather the pistachio spread on the bottom pieces, about 2 tablespoons per sandwich. Lay the warmed pork on the pistachio spread, then add the anchovies and mint leaves. Hit each sandwich with a squeeze of lemon. Drizzle the other pieces of bread with a teaspoon of oil each and, if you like, spread a mashed garlic clove on each one. Close up the sandwiches, cut in half, and serve.

PORK SANDWICHES *with* AIOLI *and* BITTER GREENS

This aioli fairly shouts garlic and is counterpoised by bitter greens, sliced pork, and lemon juice. It's a prime example of strong flavors that leap out when you first bite into them and then meld together in the crucible of your palate, combining and crescendo-ing with each chew. If you like, you can skip the bread and serve this as a main course; in that case, you'll want 4 slices of pork per person.

Note: *You will have aioli left over. Use it to dress vegetables, cold chicken, lamb, or fish. It's okay for a day or two, but any longer and it doesn't maintain the same powerful yet rounded taste.*

SERVES 4

MAKE THE ROSEMARY OIL

2 tablespoons fresh rosemary leaves
1 cup canola or grapeseed oil

If you have a laser thermometer, heat the oil to 180°F in a small saucepan. Add the rosemary leaves and steep in the oil for 20 minutes, monitoring the temperature so it stays at 180°F. You can do this in the oven if you don't have a laser thermometer: Heat the oven to 180°F. Combine the rosemary and oil in a small baking dish and heat/steep in the oven for 20 minutes. Cool the oil to room temperature.

MAKE THE AIOLI

1 large egg yolk
2 tablespoons water
2 garlic cloves (or as many as you want), grated or minced
Pinch of cayenne pepper
Pinch of kosher salt
Rosemary Oil (you can also make this with 1 cup oil from Oil-Poached Garlic, page 20, or olive oil)
15 oil-cured black olives, pitted and chopped

Combine the egg yolk, water, garlic, cayenne, and salt in a food processor and blend well. With the processor running, slowly drizzle in the oil in a very thin stream until the mixture just begins to thicken, then add the rest of the oil in a slightly thicker stream and run until the aioli reaches a consistency that is slightly looser than Hellmann's. Add the olives and pulse. Scrape down the sides and transfer to a bowl.

PUT IT ALL TOGETHER

A small handful of arugula, watercress, or other bitter greens
Juice of 1 lemon
2 tablespoons olive oil
Kosher salt
1 baguette or other long loaf
½ cup Aioli
8 (¼- to ½-inch-thick) slices Pork-Shoulder Pot Roast (page 52; the pork should be cold for optimal slicing)

Toss the greens with the lemon juice and olive oil, then sprinkle lightly with salt. Split the baguette and cut into sandwich-sized pieces (you be the judge). Toast or warm the bread in the oven if you like.

Smear the cut sides of the bread with the aioli. Lay the pork on the bottom pieces and top with the bitter greens. Close up the sandwiches and serve.

A SERIOUS PORK MELT

It is a well-known fact that melted cheese can make any sandwich memorable. For this one, I like a strong-flavored cheese such as raclette or Fontina that adds its own funk to the pork's. Although I love European cheeses, cheesemakers from Vermont, Wisconsin, and California—to name just three states—are now making superb cheese. Support your local cheese!

This recipe calls for pickled raisins. Pickling adds tangy acidity to the natural sweetness of raisins. I also use these raisins in salads and with roasted lamb and braised radicchio or cabbage.

SERVES 4

MAKE THE PICKLED RAISINS

1 cup raisins
1 cup white or red wine vinegar
½ cup water
2 tablespoons sugar
1 teaspoon crushed red pepper flakes
1 tablespoon olive oil
Pinch of kosher salt

Combine all the ingredients in a medium saucepan and bring to boil, then remove from the heat and let steep for 20 minutes.

Preheat the oven to 400°F.

WARM THE PORK

8 (¼-inch-thick) slices Pork-Shoulder Pot Roast (page 52; the pork should be cold for optimal slicing)
¼ cup reserved pork jus from the pot roast
4 fresh sage leaves, chopped

Put the pork in a large skillet, add the jus and sage, and warm over medium-low heat.

PUT IT ALL TOGETHER

2 tablespoons Oil-Poached Shallots (page 20), plus ¼ cup of the oil or olive oil
1 to 2 loaves rustic bread or 4 rolls (focaccia and baguettes are nice, as are Portuguese rolls), split
2 tablespoons Pickled Raisins, plus ¼ cup of the pickling liquid
8 thin slices Fontina, raclette, Morbier, or other funky semisoft cheese
Warmed pork
⅓ cup hazelnuts, toasted (page 17) and crushed with the flat of a chef's knife

Spread the shallot oil on the cut sides of the bread or rolls. Dab a few teaspoons of the pickling liquid on each bottom piece. Lay the shallots on the bottoms, followed by 2 slices of cheese on each one, and then stack the pork on top. Spread the hazelnuts and raisins on top of the pork. Close the sandwiches up and wrap in foil—the foil can act as a press if you wrap them very tightly, so go ahead and snug them up like super-swaddled babies. Put the sandwiches on a baking sheet and warm in the oven until they are heated through and the cheese is melted, about 15 minutes. Cut in half and serve.

ROASTED RACK of LAMB

ROASTED RACK *of* LAMB

BASIC RECIPE

When I was growing up, my Grandma Hazel gave me a lot of ribbing for my dislike of vegetables and my love of (very expensive!) lamb chops. She was the only one in the family who cooked them for me, and she did so nearly every time I visited her.

I like the big eight-bone racks that my butcher gets from Colorado. They're larger than racks from New Zealand or Iceland, which are more commonly found in markets. Bottom line: Use what you can get. If you have any say in the matter, don't have the racks Frenched, although many markets automatically add this allegedly gourmet touch, where the meat and fat are scraped away from the long bone of each rib. This practice is somewhat mystifying to me, because the meat on the "handle" is sublime. Likewise, my idea of a properly butchered lamb rack has a fat cap about ¼ inch thick. It renders as appealingly as the skin on a duck breast. Go ahead and gnaw on the handle meat and the crisp fat—enjoy life!

SERVES 4

1 (2½- to 3½-pound) lamb rack or 2 smaller racks (about 1½ pounds each)
2 to 3 teaspoons kosher salt (about 1 teaspoon per pound)
2 tablespoons canola or grapeseed oil

Preheat the oven to 400°F. Set a rack in a roasting pan or on a baking sheet.

Put the lamb rack(s) in a large bowl and shower with the salt. Then rub the lamb all over the bowl until the salt has been completely absorbed.

Oil a large heavy-bottomed skillet and heat over medium heat until hot. Lay the lamb in the pan, fat cap down, and cook until the fat cap is golden, 3 to 8 minutes. Your goal is to render out the fat and develop a crispy, golden crust. It may get a bit smoky; an open window and/or exhaust fan will solve the problem.

Place the lamb, fat cap down, on the metal rack set in the roasting pan, put it in the oven, and set the timer for 10 minutes. When the timer goes off, flip the rack(s) so that the fat cap is up and check the internal temperature. You are looking for a temperature of 120°F so when you pull the meat from the oven, you'll have medium-rare. Small racks may take as little as 5 more minutes; a larger rack will need longer, as much as 20 minutes.

Keep checking the internal temperature periodically. A skewer inserted into the center of the meat should feel quite warm but not burning hot when you remove it and press it to your lip.

Let the lamb rest for at least 10 minutes, or as long as several hours, with the fat side up for half the time and then fat side down. This lets the meat relax and allows the heat to be distributed through it more evenly, giving you a wall-to-wall medium rare. To serve after the lamb has rested, reheat in a preheated 375°F oven for 5 minutes.

To serve, cut down between the rib bones to separate the chops. Arrange in a messy tangle on a platter.

LAMB RACK *with* TAHINI SAUCE *and* FRESH MINT

God knows what you'll find at home in my fridge on a given day, but it's likely there will be some tahini and some olives, maybe a spicy pickle or some preserved lemons. And there is always hazelnuts or almonds. This recipe or a cousin of it often finds its way to my table.

SERVES 4

COOK THE ROASTED RACK OF LAMB (OPPOSITE)

Set aside to rest.

MAKE THE TAHINI SAUCE (PAGE 161)

FRY THE MINT LEAVES

1 cup canola or grapeseed oil
1 cup fresh mint leaves, torn if large

Set a strainer over a heatproof bowl. Heat the oil to 350°F in a small saucepan. Add the mint. The oil will bubble rapidly as water escapes from the mint leaves, then the bubbles will subside just as rapidly. When they do, drain the mint in the strainer and lay the crisped mint leaves on a paper towel.

PUT IT ALL TOGETHER

Tahini Sauce
Roasted Rack of Lamb
1/3 cup oil-cured black olives, pitted and roughly chopped
1/2 Preserved Lemon (page 22), pulp removed and discarded, rind chopped
2 jarred or canned pickled jalapeños, chopped
1 cup hazelnuts or almonds, toasted (page 17), crushed
Fried mint leaves

Reheat the lamb in a preheated 375°F oven for 5 minutes.

Smear the tahini sauce on a platter. Slice the lamb into individual chops and arrange in a messy tangle on the platter. Scatter the olives, preserved lemon, jalapeños, and nuts all over. Finish with the mint.

LAMB RACK *with* STUFFED ARTICHOKES

I have long regarded it as an act of Providence that the life cycles of lambs and artichokes converge in the spring. No doubt that is why the nations along the shore of the Mediterranean all have a recipe or two that marries earthy artichokes with delicate young lamb.

SERVES 4

COOK THE ROASTED RACK OF LAMB (PAGE 66)

Set aside to rest.

MEANWHILE, COOK THE ARTICHOKES

2 large artichokes (about 12 ounces each)

Peel off the tough outer leaves of the artichokes. Then cut off the top third of each artichoke. There will still be a few small pointy outer leaves; trim off the pointy tops. Lop off the stems. Place the artichokes stem end up in a steamer basket set in a pot filled with ½ inch of water. Cover with a tight-fitting lid and steam until a sharp knife easily pierces the stem end of the artichokes, 20 to 30 minutes. Set the artichokes on a plate lined with a dishtowel and let them cool a bit.

When the artichokes are cool enough to handle, spread open the centers and, using a sharp spoon (or a grapefruit spoon), scoop out the soft, pale inner leaves and the hairy chokes; discard.

Preheat the oven to 300°F.

MAKE THE STUFFING

3 tablespoons canola or grapeseed oil
2 (¾-inch-thick) slices rustic bread (whole wheat is great)
A 4-ounce chunk of Parmigiano-Reggiano, broken into small chunks
1 teaspoon ground cumin
Pinch of cayenne pepper
Grated zest of 1 lemon

Heat the oil in a large skillet, then add the bread and fry, turning once, until mahogany brown, 2 to 3 minutes per side. Transfer to a baking sheet and place in the oven for 10 to 12 minutes, until the bread is fairly well dried. Let cool.

When the bread is cool enough to handle, break it up into pieces and pulse in a food processor until the crumbs are the size of pearls. Remove the bread and add the Parmesan chunks to the processor. Run until the cheese bits are about the same size as the bread crumbs. Toss the bread, cheese, cumin, cayenne, and lemon zest together.

STUFF THE ARTICHOKES

Working with one artichoke at a time, gently pull open the leaves and press some of the stuffing between the layers, then fill the cavity with more stuffing. Save a little bit of the stuffing to sprinkle on the chops and the platter.

PUT IT ALL TOGETHER

Roasted Rack of Lamb
Stuffed Artichokes
Oil from Oil-Poached Garlic or Shallots (see page 20) or olive oil for drizzling
4 lemon cheeks (page 163)

Reheat the lamb in a preheated 375°F oven for 5 minutes. Remove from the oven. Slice the rack into individual chops.

Arrange the artichokes and lamb chops on a platter or individual plates. Drizzle the oil over everything and sprinkle the reserved stuffing over. Garnish with the lemon cheeks.

LAMB RACK *with* MINT CHIMICHURRI

My Grandma Hazel always had a jar of mint jelly in her fridge. The sauce here has the mintiness of old-time jelly with the flavors of chimichurri, a condiment that is found in the saddlebag of every self-respecting gaucho and at every backyard barbecue of Buenos Aires urbanites who like to imagine themselves gauchos for a day.

SERVES 4

COOK THE ROASTED RACK OF LAMB (PAGE 66)

Set aside to rest.

MEANWHILE, MAKE THE MINT CHIMICHURRI

1 cup fresh mint leaves, minced
½ cup olive oil
2 Oil-Poached Garlic cloves (page 20), minced
1 garlic clove, grated or minced and mashed to a puree with some salt (page 70)
¼ teaspoon ground cumin
⅛ teaspoon cayenne pepper or crushed red pepper flakes
1 tablespoon red wine vinegar

Stir the mint, olive oil, poached garlic, fresh garlic, cumin, and cayenne or pepper flakes together in a small bowl and set aside to rest for a while to mellow a bit. Add the vinegar just before serving.

PUT IT ALL TOGETHER

Roasted Rack of Lamb
Mint Chimichurri

Reheat the lamb in a preheated 375°F oven for 5 minutes.

Slice and make a tangle of the chops on a platter, haphazardly angling up the bones. Dole out some of the chimichurri all over the chops. Pass the remainder around at the table.

HOW TO PUREE GARLIC WITH A KNIFE

I learned this trick from a talented and colorful German fellow named George who was a sous chef at Seeger's in Atlanta. Basically, you mash the garlic on top of a small pile of kosher salt with the flat of a chef's knife. Then finely chop it, scatter a little more salt over the garlic, and continue mashing and chopping. The salt's coarseness acts like sandpaper, transforming the garlic into a puree.

Proven fact: slugs and salt-rimmed margaritas do <u>not</u> mix well.

LAMB RACK *with* TOMATILLOS *and* FETA CRUMBLE

Here I've taken medium-rare lamb racks, which I more often associate with British or French flavors, and nestled them into a sauce that is more commonly eaten with the slow-braised or long-roasted lamb and goat dishes of Central American cuisines. As it turns out, shorter-cooked lamb racks pair wonderfully with pureed mildly spicy jalapeños and tart tomatillos.

SERVES 4

COOK THE ROASTED RACK OF LAMB (PAGE 66)

Set aside to rest.

MEANWHILE, MAKE THE TOMATILLO SAUCE

4 medium tomatillos, papery skin removed and rinsed
1 jalapeño
2 tablespoons oil from Oil-Poached Garlic or Shallots (page 20) or olive oil
1 teaspoon kosher salt
Pinch of crushed red pepper flakes (optional)

Put the tomatillos and jalapeño on a baking sheet or in an ovenproof skillet. Roast in the 400°F oven until the tomatillos have softened and given up some liquid and the jalapeño has colored a little, 20 to 25 minutes. Remove from the oven and let cool slightly.

Cut the stem off the jalapeño and put the chili in a blender, along with the tomatillos, oil, and salt. Run until you have a smooth puree. Check the spiciness, and add the crushed red pepper if you want to dial it up. Set aside.

MAKE THE FETA CRUMBLE

1 cup crumbled feta (about 4 ounces)
1/3 cup whole almonds, toasted (page 17) and crushed
1/4 cup fresh oregano leaves or 1 to 2 tablespoons dried oregano
2 teaspoons nigella seeds (sometimes called black onion or black cumin seeds; optional)

Mix together the feta, almonds, oregano, and nigella, if using, in a bowl; set aside.

PUT IT ALL TOGETHER

Roasted Rack of Lamb
Tomatillo Sauce
Feta Crumble
1 tablespoon oil from Oil-Poached Garlic or Shallots (page 20) or olive oil

Reheat the lamb in a preheated 375°F oven for 5 minutes.

Smear some of the tomatillo sauce over a platter; pass the rest of the sauce at the table. Slice the rack into individual chops and make a tall messy tangle of them on top of the sauce. Strew the feta crumble over them and drizzle with the oil.

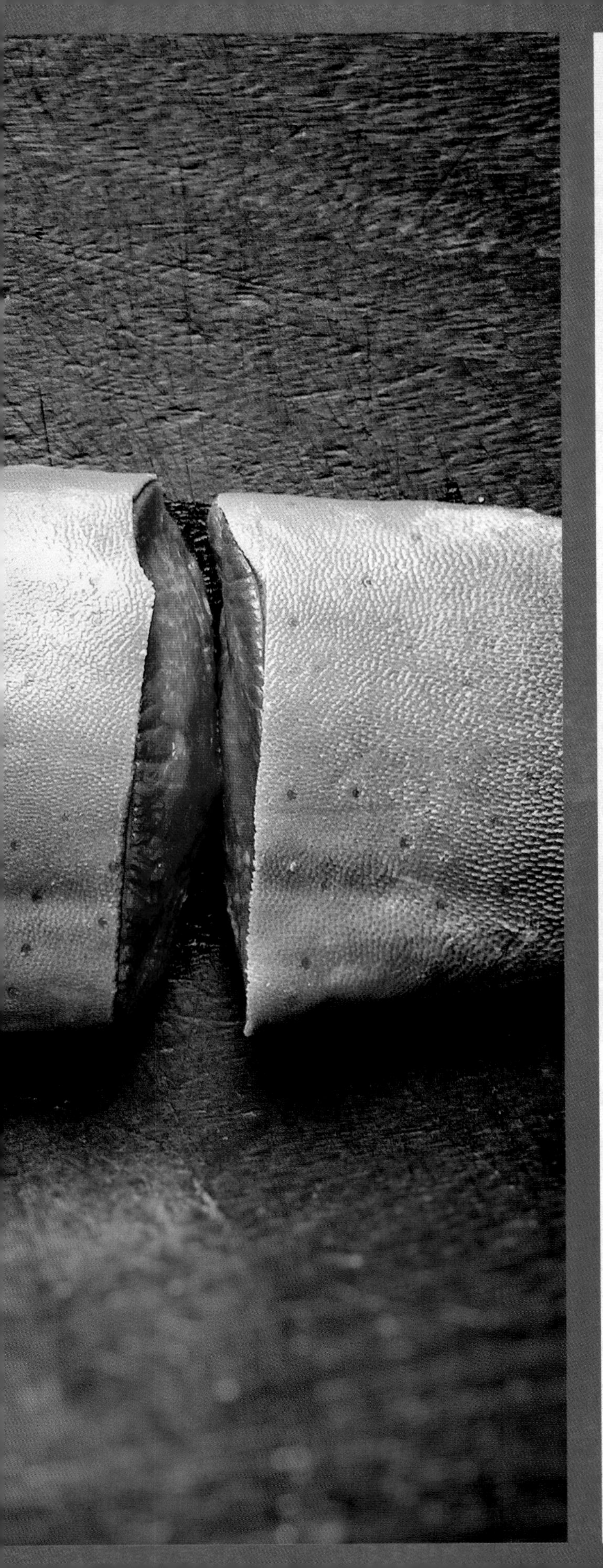

BRAISED BEEF TONGUE

BRAISED BEEF TONGUE

BASIC RECIPE

I found that long simmering—in other words, a braise—brings out the tongue's magic. No less delightful than braised beef short ribs, lamb shank, osso buco, or goat neck, beef tongue has smooth and buttery succulence and a deep beefy flavor that borders on psychedelic. The recipe can also be made with veal, lamb, or pork tongue; timing will vary, depending on the weight.

Note: *Start this recipe at least 24 hours ahead so the flavors from the braising liquid can infuse the tongue.*

MAKES ENOUGH FOR SEVERAL MEALS; *refer to the recipes that follow*

Preheat the oven to 300°F.

MAKE THE SPICE SACHET

2 bay leaves
1 tablespoon coriander seeds
1 tablespoon fennel seeds
1 teaspoon crushed red pepper flakes
A few sprigs of fresh thyme

Wrap the bay leaves, coriander and fennel seeds, red pepper flakes, and thyme in a square of cheesecloth and tie up with kitchen twine.

BRAISE THE TONGUE

1 garlic head, halved horizontally
1 small-medium onion, quartered
1 fennel bulb, stalk, fronds, and all, quartered or roughly chopped
1 beef tongue (about 3 pounds), cut into 3 or 4 pieces
2 tablespoons kosher salt

Put the garlic, onion, and fennel in a Dutch oven or other large pot with a lid. Add the spice sachet. Place the tongue in the pot and cover with water by 2 inches (about 2 quarts). Add the salt and bring the liquid to a simmer.

Transfer the pot to the oven and cook until the tongue is super tender, about 3 hours. When the tongue is done (check all the pieces; they will vary in thickness), transfer it to a platter and let cool slightly. Strain the braising liquid and return it to the pot.

When the tongue is cool enough to handle, peel off the tough outer covering. Return the tongue to the liquid. Let cool, then refrigerate for at least 24 hours or for up to a week so the flavors from the braising liquid really penetrate the tongue.

TESTING FOR DONENESS

Many cooks—pros just as much as amateurs—overcook braised meats because of loaded terms like "falling off the bone" or "meltingly tender." The best way to determine doneness in any braised meat is to stick it with something. I use a metal Japanese chopstick that's tapered and looks like an elongated icepick. A kitchen thermometer also works great, or you can use a paring knife. Whatever you use, when the meat is done, your probe should slide in and out with no resistance.

They could stare at each other for hours.

TONGUE *with* TOMATILLO SAUCE

A few years ago, I visited Oaxaca, a picturesque colonial city that has one of the richest culinary traditions in Mexico—from its insanely complex *mole negro* to the austere *sopa de guias* (a soup made with zucchini flowers, leaves, and vines, as well as zucchini). Oaxacans use a tremendous variety of chilies for flavor, for spiciness, for texture. Tomatillos brighten the dish with their characteristic tanginess.

Note: *Pasilla, guajillo, and ancho chilies have big flavor but not as much spicy heat as more thermonuclear chilies such as habanero or Scotch bonnet; their heat is warm and subtle. If you want a hotter dish, use more chilies.*

SERVES 4

MAKE THE SAUCE

3 dried chilies, such as pasilla, guajillo, or ancho (see Note)

4 cups water

2 medium tomatillos, papery skin removed and rinsed

1 tablespoon oil from Oil-Poached Garlic or Shallots (page 20) or olive oil

1 tablespoon red or white vinegar

1/2 cup almonds, toasted (page 17) and crushed with the flat of a chef's knife

1 garlic clove, peeled

1/2 teaspoon kosher salt, or to taste

About 1 tablespoon olive oil or water if needed

Preheat the oven to 400°F.

Put the chilies in a saucepan, add the water, and simmer until they are soft, about 30 minutes.

Meanwhile, toss the tomatillos with the oil and roast on a baking sheet pan or in a cast-iron skillet until a bit of tan blooms their skins and they have "relaxed" (softened but not yet turned to complete mush), about 20 minutes. Set aside.

When the chilies are soft, remove them with a slotted spoon, let cool, and pull off their stems. Strain the cooking liquid. Put the chilies in a blender and run, adding the vinegar and enough of the cooking liquid, bit by bit, to make a loose puree. Pour the puree into a strainer set over a bowl, pushing it through with a spatula or wooden spoon to remove the bits of skin. (No need to wash the blender.)

Add the tomatillos, almonds, garlic, and salt to the blender and run until the almonds have pretty much disappeared into the juices. Return ½ cup of the pureed chilies to the blender and run until nicely incorporated. Taste for spiciness, and add more of the puree if you want it spicier. The sauce should be as thick as marinara sauce. If the peppers are spicy, but the sauced seems too thick, skip the extra puree and adjust the consistency with a tablespoon of oil or water instead. Season with more salt if necessary. Save any extra puree to pass at the table, or refrigerate or freeze; it is a great all-purpose condiment for anything grilled.

PUT IT ALL TOGETHER

Sauce

½-inch-thick slices Braised Tongue (page 76; the tongue should be cold for optimal slicing), 2 or 3 slices per person

Olive oil

A handful of watercress

Kosher salt

¼ cup almonds, toasted (page 17) and crushed with the flat of a chef's knife

Warm the sauce. Meanwhile, heat the tongue by searing the slices in a lightly oiled skillet, no more than a minute on each side; you're just looking for a little color on the meat. Dress the watercress ever lightly with about 1 tablespoon olive oil and a little salt.

Smear the sauce on a platter and plop the tongue on top. Strew the watercress around and sprinkle the crushed almonds over all. Drizzle with a little olive oil. If you have extra chili puree, pass it around for the heat seekers at the table.

TONGUE *with* GRIBICHE

Gribiche, traditionally served with tongue, sounds fancy, but it's just chopped pickles, herbs, and hard-boiled eggs mixed with oil and lemon juice to make a sauce. My early summer gribiche has chive blossoms and all manner of fabulousness from the garden. In the winter, I pare it down to the herbs that look good in the market. Some gribiches are emulsified, but this one isn't, so don't think you've messed up if it separates. The story of my gribiche started out in grad school, when someone gave me a jar of spicy pickled okra. Apparently it's quite common in Texas, but for me it was a new and wonderful food. I was gobsmacked and wrote a gushing fan letter to the pickle makers in Texas, who replied with a complimentary case of the stuff. It lasted through two years of grad school. Don't obsess about finding pickled okra. Use what you have on hand or can get easily, like cornichons, capers, or even dill pickles, rather than buying a jar of something that will stay in the dark recesses of the fridge for months.

Note: *I recommend a mix of herbs, but keep in mind that herbs like tarragon and oregano are stronger than parsley, so don't mix them in equal volumes. Mix by strength.*

SERVES 4

MAKE THE GRIBICHE

2 large eggs

2 tablespoons brined capers, drained and finely chopped

½ cup pickled okra or cornichons (see above), drained and finely chopped

1 cup mixed fresh herb leaves, such as tarragon, chervil, flat-leaf parsley, dill, and/or chives (see Note), finely chopped

Juice of 1 lemon

3 tablespoons oil from Oil-Poached Garlic or Shallots (page 20) or olive oil

Boil the eggs for 9 minutes as directed on page 241. Cool, then peel and finely chop.

Combine the eggs, capers, okra or cornichons, and herbs in a bowl. Add the lemon juice and oil, and stir with a fork or a spoon. Check for deliciousness and set aside.

MAKE THE GREENS AND HERB SALAD

1 cup mixed fresh herb leaves (the same mix as above)

2 cups mizuna, watercress, friseé, or purslane—whatever you can get your hands on

Combine the herbs and greens in a bowl.

PUT IT ALL TOGETHER

16 (½-inch-thick) slices Braised Tongue (page 76; the tongue should be chilled for optimal slicing)

Gribiche

Greens and Herb Salad

2 tablespoons olive oil, plus more for drizzling

Juice of 1 large lemon

Kosher salt

If you like, warm the tongue in a 350°F oven for about 5 minutes, or until warmed through.

Smear the gribiche on a platter. Dress the salad with the olive oil, lemon, and salt to taste and scatter here and there on the platter, saving a bit for the final touch. Scatter the slices of tongue all around. Finish with the rest of the salad and a few drizzles of olive oil.

SPICY TONGUE DAUBE *with* ROOTS *and* PRUNES

When I was an art student living in rural Vermont, trying to figure out how to feed myself with no help from grown-ups, I often resorted to Dinty Moore. I've never lost my love for beef stew, although I have since set my culinary sights a bit higher than good old Dinty. A well-executed daube—a long-simmered Provençal beef stew—calls to my inner Francophile. The traditional recipe uses chuck, which I find to be problematic: It's cut from a section of beef that has a number of different muscles that want to cook at different rates. If you cook one part correctly, you can be sure that another part is off the mark. Tongue, however, cooks uniformly and slices into lovely stew-sized pieces, making it an ideal choice for a daube.

The method for cooking the tongue is the same as in the basic recipe, but I've changed up the spice mix and braising vegetables a bit. Serve with a loaf of crusty bread that has been warmed in the oven, or brown rice, farro, or barley to soak up the juices.

Note: *Be sure to cook the tongue at least a day ahead so that the flavors from the braise can thoroughly infuse it.*

SERVES 4

Preheat the oven to 300°F.

MAKE THE SPICE SACHET

1 ½ tablespoons cumin seeds
1 ½ tablespoons coriander seeds
1 ½ tablespoons fenugreek seeds
1 ½ tablespoons whole fennel seeds
1 tablespoon crushed red pepper flakes
2 teaspoons cardamom pods
3 bay leaves

Wrap all the spices and bay leaves in a square of cheesecloth and tie it up tightly with kitchen twine.

BRAISE THE TONGUE

1 onion, roughly chopped
1 garlic head, cut horizontally in half
1 beefsteak tomato, chopped, or 1 cup good canned tomatoes
2 dried medium-hot chilies (such as guajillo, pasilla, ancho, or chile de árbol)
1 small beef tongue (2 pounds)
2 tablespoons kosher salt

Put the onion, garlic, tomato, and chilies on a Dutch oven or other large pot. Add the spice sachet. Place the tongue in the pot and cover with water by 2 inches. Add the salt and bring the liquid to a simmer.

Transfer the pot to the oven and cook until the tongue is super tender, about 3 hours. When the tongue is done, transfer to a platter and let cool slightly. Strain the braising liquid and return it to the pot.

When the tongue is cool enough to handle, peel it and cut it into pieces about the size of a small plum. Return the chunks to the strained cooking liquid, let cool, and refrigerate for at least 24 hours (or up to a week, getting a little more delicious every day).

CONTINUED

MAKE THE DAUBE VEGETABLES

8 tablespoons (1 stick) unsalted butter or, better yet, ½ cup fat from the braised tongue

8 ounces mushrooms (maitake, king trumpet, or shiitake—your choice)

1 fennel bulb with stalks, cut into ¼-inch-thick slices

8 ounces carrots, cut into ⅜-inch-thick coins

1 small red onion, cut into ¼-inch-thick slices

¼ cup balsamic vinegar

2 cups white or red wine

2 cups reserved braising liquid from the tongue

½ cup pitted prunes, halved

Kosher salt

Heat the butter or fat in a large pot over medium-high heat. Sauté the mushrooms until they have browned a bit but are not caramelized, a matter of minutes. Remove the mushrooms with a slotted spoon and set aside. Add the fennel, carrots, and onion to the pot and cook for 4 minutes, or until they have lightly browned. Pour off the fat.

Add the balsamic vinegar to the pot and cook for 2 minutes, then add the wine and boil until the alcohol cooks off, about 3 minutes. Lower the heat to simmer, add the tongue braising liquid, sautéed mushrooms, and prunes and cook until all the vegetables are soft, 15 to 20 minutes. Check the seasoning and add a little salt if needed.

PUT IT ALL TOGETHER

Braised Tongue chunks

Daube vegetables

¼ cup fresh flat-leaf parsley, chervil, tarragon, or chives, or a mixture, chopped

2 tablespoons unsalted butter

A splash of good red wine vinegar if necessary

Add the tongue to the pot with the vegetables and gently reheat it. Remove from the heat and stir in the chopped herbs and butter. Taste the liquid. If it would benefit from a touch more acidity, add a splash of vinegar.

TONGUE *with* LIGHTLY PICKLED VEGETABLES *and* SOUR CREAM

Whether braised, slow-roasted, or boiled, beef likes pickles—something tangy or sharp to wake up the palate between bites. And the combination of beef, pickles, and sour cream is enshrined in Eastern European food traditions. This pickle is my version of Italian giardiniera salad. It is also superb with grilled fish, roast or fried chicken, or a plate of charcuterie.

MAKE THE PICKLED VEGETABLES

If you don't have all these spices, it's okay to skip one or two of them.

1 tablespoon fennel seeds
1 tablespoon coriander seeds
1 tablespoon cumin seeds
1 tablespoon fenugreek seeds
4 cups white wine vinegar
4 cups water
¼ cup kosher salt
¼ cup sugar
2 or 3 bay leaves
½ small head cauliflower, broken down into bite-sized pieces
2 medium carrots, cut into slices a little less than ¼ inch thick
4 celery stalks, cut into ¼-inch-thick slices on the bias
1 small onion, thinly sliced
1 fennel bulb, trimmed and thinly sliced
2 medium beefsteak tomatoes, cut into 8 wedges each, or 1 pint cherry tomatoes, halved
6 garlic cloves, cut into ¼-inch-thick slices
1 teaspoon crushed red pepper flakes

Wrap the fennel, coriander, cumin, and fenugreek seeds in a square of cheesecloth and tie up the sachet firmly. Combine the vinegar, water, salt, sugar, and bay leaves in a large saucepan, add the sachet, and bring to a simmer. Then reduce the heat slightly and simmer for 15 minutes.

Add all the vegetables to the simmering liquid and simmer for 4 minutes. Remove from the heat, add the garlic and red pepper flakes, and let cool to room temperature.

Transfer the vegetables and brine to a container and refrigerate for a minimum of 24 hours before serving. (You won't use all of the vegetables for this recipe, but they will keep well in the fridge.)

SLICE THE BRAISED TONGUE

12 to 18 ounces chilled Braised Beef Tongue (page 76)

Cut the chilled tongue into 12 chunks (1 to 1½ ounces each), bigger than bite-sized but smaller than a mouthful.

PUT IT ALL TOGETHER

2 cups Pickled Vegetables
Braised Tongue chunks
Olive oil
1 cup sour cream
1 cup fresh flat-leaf parsley leaves, chopped or left whole

Warm the pickled vegetables in a saucepan. Meanwhile, warm the tongue chunks in a lightly oiled skillet, turning occasionally, to slightly crisp the edges, just a few minutes.

Smear the sour cream over a platter and top with the tongue. Remove the pickled vegetables from the saucepan with a slotted spoon and arrange over the tongue. Scatter the parsley over all.

TONGUE REUBEN *with* FRESH KRAUT

A classic Reuben is made with corned beef, Swiss cheese, and sauerkraut sandwiched between two slices of rye bread slathered with Russian dressing. Here I replace the corned beef with sliced tongue, skip the dressing, and add fresh kraut made with savoy cabbage. I suggest finding a funky alpine cheese like raclette (there's a good one made by Springbrook Farm in Vermont called Reading Raclette). I like to melt the cheese (the Reuben is really just a souped-up grilled cheese, after all) using both the stovetop and the oven; this is a thick sandwich that needs to be thoroughly warmed. Using the oven dramatically decreases the probability that you'll burn the bread in the pan, the chief pitfall of a grilled cheese sandwich.

SERVES 4

MAKE THE FRESH KRAUT

4 tablespoons (½ stick) unsalted butter
1 medium onion, thinly sliced
3 to 4 cups thinly sliced savoy cabbage
2 teaspoons kosher salt
1 teaspoon ground caraway
2 tablespoons white wine vinegar

Melt the butter in a large skillet over medium heat. Sauté the onion for 3 to 5 minutes, until softened but not browned. Add the cabbage, sprinkle with the salt, and stir to wilt, about 1 minute. Add the caraway and vinegar, toss, and cook for another minute or so. You want the cabbage to remain somewhat crunchy. Remove from the heat.

PUT IT ALL TOGETHER

8 ounces cheese, such as raclette, Gruyère, or another similar funky semisoft cheese, thinly sliced
8 slices rye bread
20 (¼-inch-thick) slices Braised Tongue (page 76; the tongue should be chilled for optimal slicing)
Fresh Kraut
4 teaspoons mustard (any kind), or to taste
2 tablespoons canola or grapeseed oil

Preheat the oven to 400°F.

Place 3 slices of cheese each on 4 slices of bread. Layer the tongue slices on top of the cheese, followed by a layer of fresh kraut, and finish each with 2 more slices of cheese. Spread the mustard on the remaining slices of bread and close up the sandwiches.

Heat the oil in a large skillet over medium heat and brown the sandwiches on both sides (if only 2 sandwiches fit in the pan, do this in batches).

To finish, transfer the sandwiches to a rack set on a baking sheet and heat in the oven until the cheese has melted and the interiors are warm, 10 to 15 minutes. Cut the sandwiches and serve.

Blumen
A night on the town

Poached Cod

POACHED COD

BASIC RECIPE

It was the height of the Norwegian summer, and the weather was spectacular. Jordana and I had traveled as far north as Kjerringøy, where we stayed with the painter Karl Erik Harr, the father of one of Frank's art school friends. He had a large property right on the sea, and a rowboat for fishing, which he offered to us.

We used hand lines: heavy fishing line wrapped around weathered chunks of wood. Each line had several hooks with faded bits of rubber for lures. We rowed out to a spot that Mr. Harr had recommended. As soon as our rigs hit bottom, *whump, whump*, cod attached themselves to every hook. We quickly amassed enough fish for dinner and rowed back to shore. Frank brought a pot down to the beach, filled it with seawater, and set it on a rustic stove.

Frank boiled the potatoes in the seawater and served them with softened shallots, parsley, salt, and butter. Then he turned down the heat under the pot, so the water was faintly simmering, and cooked our fish. He had been talking about boiled cod for the entire trip, and it hardly needs be said that the term "boiled cod" held little allure for me. I pictured a huge pot at a rolling boil with the cod being vigorously tossed about and broken up. It was only when I saw him cooking that I realized that "boiled cod" was a quirk of his English vocabulary, and what he meant was something much gentler.

The cod was spectacular. We drank aquavit and cold Norwegian beer. Afterward, both Jordana and I found ourselves very sleepy. Norwegians believe that cod is a soporific. We found it so and took a long nap.

Note: *Kombu, available online and in many markets, is dried kelp, seaweed. Japanese chefs have used it for centuries to enhance the savoriness of cooked food. One package will last a long while.*

SERVES 4

SALT THE COD

1 ½ pounds cod fillet, cut into 8 portions
1 teaspoon kosher salt

You want to salt the cod about an hour before you cook it (but it can even go overnight). This tightens the flesh a bit, so it holds together better when you poach it, and it adds the saltiness you would get from seawater. Put the cod on a plate, sprinkle all over with the salt, and refrigerate.

POACH THE COD

8 cups water
2 (6-inch) squares kombu (optional)

Bring the water and the kombu, if using, to a simmer in a large pot over high heat. Add the cod. When the cold fish hits the water, the temperature will drop, likely to around 160°F—an ideal poaching temperature. You really don't want to go much higher than this. *Bear in mind that poaching water shouldn't bubble, like a simmer.* Reduce the heat as necessary. The best way to monitor the temperature is with a laser thermometer (see page 16), but you can use an instant-read or candy thermometer. At 160°F, a piece of fish from the tail end of the fillet, which is relatively thin, will cook in 4 to 5 minutes; a thicker piece (2 inches) might take closer to 10 minutes. You'll know the fish is done if a cake tester or skewer (or thermometer) meets no resistance when you insert it. When I remove the cake tester, I press it directly above my upper lip to check: It should feel warm (not hot, not room temperature, but warm). The cod will flake a little if it's fully cooked, which gives you an opportunity to check the color in the middle of the fish; the flesh should be opaque. It's okay to feel these flakes with your finger to confirm warmness. (As much as possible, I try to take the mystery out of ascertaining doneness: The more senses you can use, the less mysterious this becomes.) With a slotted spoon, transfer the cod to a platter.

PUT IT ALL TOGETHER

Poached cod
Olive oil for drizzling
Flaky sea salt
Minced fresh herb(s) of your choice

Serve the cod with a drizzle of olive oil, some flaky salt, and fresh herb(s).

COD SALAD *with* TARRAGON SAUCE *and* BOILED EGGS

Eggs and cod are a time-honored marriage of textures and tastes. The starting point for this dish was the "grand aioli" of Provence, which features a robust aioli with crudités and cod. Here I've simply combined all of the flavors of that sauce but edited out the garlic. When you serve this, be sure to flake the cod a little so the sauce can flavor as much of the fish as possible. I like this with boiled new potatoes or green beans, but here, as elsewhere, let the market be your guide.

SERVES 4

SALT THE COD

1 ½ pounds cod fillet, cut into 8 portions
1 teaspoon kosher salt

Salt the cod as directed on page 90.

MEANWHILE, MAKE THE TARRAGON SAUCE

2 tablespoons minced shallots
3 tablespoons olive oil
1 ½ tablespoons roughly chopped capers
1 tablespoon minced fresh tarragon
1 teaspoon Dijon mustard
Juice of ½ lemon
1 or 2 anchovy fillets

Cook the shallots in the oil in a small saucepan for 3 minutes. They should still have a little crunch, but the cooking will dial back the raw oniony sharpness. Transfer to a bowl and stir in the capers, tarragon, mustard, lemon juice, and anchovies.

COOK THE 6-MINUTE EGGS

6 large eggs

Boil the eggs in a large pot for 6 minutes as directed on page 241. Peel the eggs.

POACH THE COD

Cook the cod as directed on page 90. Transfer to a platter and set aside cod to cool briefly. Leave the poaching water on the stove.

PUT IT ALL TOGETHER

6-Minute Eggs
Tarragon Sauce
1 brimming cup mixed fresh flat-leaf parsley and dill leaves
Poached Cod

Rewarm the eggs for a minute in the poaching water.

Meanwhile, drizzle about a third of the sauce here and there over a platter. Roughly chop the eggs, taking a couple of passes through each one with a knife. Arrange half of the eggs on the platter. Scatter a little of the parsley and dill around. Add the fish to the platter. Hopefully it will flake apart as you do this, but if it doesn't, help it along so that there are pieces of cod scattered here and there. Add the rest of the eggs and parsley and then drizzle and dab the remainder of the dressing all around. If it looks chaotic, you've done it right.

COD *and* MUSSELS *in* SPICY FUMET

I traveled to Marseille some years ago; it was a solo trip and an enlightening one. A port city just across the Mediterranean from North Africa, Marseille is a melting pot of peoples and cultures. I had fantasized about fish markets and quaint restaurants, but what I found instead was a modern port and lots of neon-signed tourist traps. Fortunately, in my off-the-beaten-track wandering, I found delicious food from Morocco, Tunisia, Algeria, and Libya. The last night in town, I ate at Le Petit Nice Passedat, a restaurant that overlooked the water. The proprietor was a local fellow and a second-generation chef. Although he had earned two Michelin stars, his bouillabaisse contained a delicious hodgepodge of fish from the local waters. Since that time, I have loved cooking my own versions of bouillabaisse with seafood from our own waters.

SERVES 4

SALT THE COD

1 ½ pounds cod fillet, cut into 8 portions
1 teaspoon kosher salt

Salt the cod as directed on page 90.

MEANWHILE, PREP THE VEGETABLES

2 tablespoons oil from Oil-Poached Garlic or Shallots (page 20) or olive oil
1 medium fennel bulb, fronds removed and reserved, bulb and stalks thinly sliced
1 red or yellow onion, thinly sliced
3 medium garlic cloves, thinly sliced
2 tablespoons tomato paste

Slick a large skillet with the oil and warm over medium-high heat. Add the sliced fennel, onions, and garlic and cook—don't brown—for a few minutes or so. When the fennel is softish to the tooth, add the tomato paste. Cook for 2 minutes, stirring frequently. Set aside.

COOK THE MUSSELS AND COD

24 plump mussels, scrubbed and debearded if necessary
½ teaspoon cayenne pepper
1 teaspoon ground cumin
1 teaspoon ground caraway
4 cups Fish Fumet (page 98) or water
Salted Cod

Combine the mussels, cayenne, cumin, caraway, and a healthy splash of the fumet in a medium pot, cover, and cook over medium-high heat for a few minutes. The mussels should open quickly; check after a minute or two. Once they open, cook for 2 more minutes. Remove the mussels to a bowl. Add the rest of the fumet, bring to just below a simmer, and add the cod. Poach the cod at around 160°F until it flakes, as directed in the basic recipe. Remove the pot from the heat.

PUT IT ALL TOGETHER

8 slices country bread or other rustic bread
1 garlic clove, halved
Vegetables
Poached Cod
Mussels and broth
½ lemon

Rub the bread with the raw garlic and briefly grill (or toast in an oiled skillet). Rewarm the vegetables.

Using a slotted spoon, scoop the cod from the broth and into wide soup plates. Quickly rewarm the mussels in the broth, then divide the vegetables, mussels, and broth among the soup plates. Garnish with the reserved fennel fronds, and spritz with a little lemon. Serve with the toast.

POACHED COD *with* GREENS *and* VEGETABLES

Cod gently poached in a beautiful fumet doesn't have the tambourines, base drums, and trumpet blares of some other preparations, but it is a perfect foil for the subtle and nuanced flavors of fresh green herbs and vegetables. Pretty much any combination of green things will do.

A word of advice here about "perfectly cooked" vegetables and an entreaty to taste them as you cook. You should cook to your taste, and your senses are the best barometer of doneness. So, if the Swiss chard has a little bite, great! If the peas are somewhat crunchy, awesome! Or, if you like your vegetables a little softer, cook them a bit longer. Please yourself, and you are sure to please others.

SERVES 4

SALT THE COD

1 ½ pounds cod fillet, cut into 8 portions
1 teaspoon kosher salt

Salt the cod as directed on page 90.

MAKE THE VEGETABLES

1 bunch Swiss chard
¼ pound sugar snap peas
¼ pound snow peas
1 leek
1 bunch asparagus (about 1 pound)
1 to 2 tablespoons oil from Oil-Poached Garlic or Shallots (page 20) or olive oil
2 garlic cloves, sliced
1 bay leaf
1 Preserved Lemon (page 22), pulp discarded and rind minced, or grated zest of 1 fresh lemon
Pinch of Aleppo pepper or crushed red pepper flakes, or to taste
1 cup Fish Fumet (page 98) or water
½ cup green peas (frozen are fine)
⅓ brimming cup fresh mint leaves, minced
2 brimming tablespoons minced fresh tarragon

Remove the ribs from the chard and cut the leaves crosswise into ribbons about ½ inch wide. Remove the "threads" from the sugar snaps and snow peas and cut lengthwise in half on a slight bias. Trim the leek, slice into thin half-moons, and rinse thoroughly. Slice the asparagus into 2-inch lengths.

Heat the oil in a large skillet or pot over medium-high heat. Add the leek, garlic, bay leaf, preserved lemon, and pepper. When the leeks and garlic are soft, 3 to 5 minutes, add the chard and a splash of the fumet or water. Cook for 2 to 3 minutes. Add the rest of the prepped vegetables, the peas, and the remaining fumet. Lower the heat and simmer for 3 to 4 minutes. Add the herbs and set aside.

POACH THE COD

2 quarts Fish Fumet (page 98) or water

While the vegetables are cooking, bring the fumet or water to a boil in a large pot, then reduce to just below a simmer. This will allow you to cook the cod while you finish the vegetables.

Poach the cod as directed on page 90.

PUT IT ALL TOGETHER

Vegetables
1/4 to 1/2 cup Fish Fumet (page 98) or water
Poached Cod
1/2 lemon

Spoon the vegetables and fumet into wide soup plates, reserving a few vegetables for garnish. Place the cod on top of the vegetables. Add 1 to 2 tablespoons fumet to each plate. Garnish with the reserved vegetables and give each plate a spritz of lemon juice.

FISH FUMET *(Fish Broth)*

In contrast to meat and chicken bones, which require longer cooking in stock, fish bones yield their goodness quickly. Bulletproof fumet has only a couple of rules: Break as many of the fish bones as possible before adding them to the pot. Bring the liquid to a simmer, then immediately lower the heat and cook at a bare simmer for no more than 30 minutes. Be vigilant about the time. Cook it any longer, and the clean aroma of a fumet develops old fish smell. It is soul crushing!

If you shop at a fish store or a market with a good fish department, ask for fish carcasses with the gills removed. Rinse under running water for a few minutes, until you no longer see any blood. Break up the carcasses into pieces using kitchen shears or a cleaver so the bones will fit tightly in a reasonable-sized pot. Make sure that you break up the spine so that the rich gelatin cooks into the fumet.

MAKES ABOUT 2 QUARTS

(as long as you are at it, you can easily double everything and freeze the extra)

1 ½ pounds or so fish carcasses (you can include the heads)
1 large fennel bulb, including stalks and fronds
1 medium onion, peeled
1 large celery stalk
Canola or grapeseed oil
1 tablespoon black peppercorns
1 tablespoon fennel seeds
2 bay leaves
1 tablespoon kosher salt
1 (750-ml) bottle white wine

Break up the fish carcasses (see headnote). Remove the stalks from the fennel bulb. Cut the fennel bulb in half lengthwise and then into ¼-inch-thick slices. Slice the stalks slightly thicker, ⅓-inch-thick pieces. Halve the onion lengthwise and cut into ¼-inch-thick slices. Slice the celery into ¼-inch-thick half-moons.

Set a large pot over medium-high heat and film with oil. Add the peppercorns, fennel seeds, bay leaves, and salt, then add the fennel, onions, and celery and cook—don't brown—for about 5 minutes. Add the wine and cook for a few minutes to evaporate the alcohol. Throw in the fish bones and add just enough water to barely submerge the ingredients. Bring to a simmer and then back off the heat a touch. The fumet should never reach a boil. You want to maintain a temperature between a hot steep and a light simmer (180°F to 200°F). Use your laser thermometer if you have one. Set a timer for 30 minutes.

When the timer goes off, immediately strain the fumet (discard the solids) and let cool. If not using it immediately, store the fumet in the refrigerator for a few days or in the freezer for longer.

BATTERED COD *with* MANGO SLAW

Moist fish in a lacy, crunchy batter has been the goal of fish frying ever since the invention of fish and chips. Beer has long been used in the batter because the bubbles and the alcohol aerate and lighten the batter as the fish fries. Then along came Heston Blumenthal, the pioneering modernist chef of the Fat Duck in England, who added vodka to the batter as well. The high alcohol content in vodka boils off even faster than beer and further lightens the crust.

Through trial and error, I ended up with this formula, which makes a light, very crispy crust for cod. But what if you don't have a bottle of vodka in your liquor cabinet? Gin combined with beer will give a similar result. I serve this with a light—i.e., non-mayonnaise—slaw accented with *amba*, which is a wonderful tangy, sharp, Middle-Eastern mango pickle (available online, as is the rice flour). Preserved Lemon (page 22) or a jarred Indian lemon pickle will work just as well.

SERVES 4

SALT THE COD

1 ½ pounds cod fillet, cut into 8 portions
½ teaspoon kosher salt

Salt the cod as directed on page 90.

MEANWHILE, MAKE THE MANGO SLAW

¼ head cabbage, cut into ¼-by-2-inch strips
½ medium red onion, thinly sliced
1 teaspoon kosher salt
1 ½ tablespoons amba (pickled mango), chopped if necessary
Juice of 1 lime
¼ Honeycrisp apple, halved, cored, and sliced into ¼-inch-thick matchsticks
½ brimming cup fresh cilantro and/or mint leaves, chopped

Toss the cabbage, onion, and salt in a bowl and set it aside for at least 20 minutes—better if you leave it for an hour to draw out the water. Drain.

Mix the amba and lime juice, add to the cabbage, and toss again. Add the apple and herbs and give everything a final toss.

MAKE THE BATTER

½ cup white rice flour, plus more for dusting
½ cup all-purpose flour
¼ heaping teaspoon baking powder
¼ teaspoon kosher salt
¼ cup vodka (see headnote)
¾ cup lager beer (your choice), or as needed

Mix the white rice flour and all-purpose flour, baking powder, and salt in a bowl. Add the vodka and beer and whisk until smooth. You may need to whisk in a little more liquid right before you fry the cod; the batter should be thicker than crepe batter but thinner than pancake batter.

CONTINUED

FRY THE COD

8 cups canola or grapeseed oil

Heat the oil to 350°F in a deep fryer or in a deep pot over medium-high heat.

Working quickly, using tongs (or, very carefully, your fingers) dip the fish one piece at a time in the batter. Then lower the battered fillet about halfway into the hot oil for about 5 seconds (real one-Mississippi, two-Mississippi seconds)—this sets the batter so that when you let go of the whole piece it doesn't sink to the bottom or stick to the other pieces. Fry the cod until golden, 2½ to 3 minutes. Using a slotted spoon, remove the fish and drain on a rack or paper towels.

PUT IT ALL TOGETHER

Mango Slaw
Battered Cod

Put a little of the slaw on a platter. Put the cod on top and garnish with the rest of the slaw.

CRISPY-SKIN FISH FILLETS

CRISPY-SKIN FISH FILLETS

BASIC RECIPE

People often ask me how to get crispy skin on a fish fillet. It seems like a magic trick, a secret of restaurant chefs, but actually, anyone can do it. The fish has to spend a little time over the fire and then finish cooking skin side down on the floor of the oven. When it comes in contact with the hot pan, the fish wants to curl, so as soon as you lay it in the pan, you must apply firm pressure to it so the skin stays flat against the bottom of the hot pan.

This technique works for salmon, black sea bass, grouper, cod, bluefish, and—in fact—most of the other fish you can lay your hands on. It takes a little doing to know exactly how long to hold the fish down before the skin will "relax," as it varies from one kind of fish to another. For example, black sea bass will require more time over high heat than an Alaskan sockeye salmon, which crisps up very quickly. You may not get perfectly crispy skin the first time you try it, but the fish will taste great anyway. After a few times, I'm sure you'll get the feel.

SERVES 4

4 (6-ounce) white fish fillets with skin (such as striper, red fish, rockfish, or snapper; see headnote), patted dry with paper towels
1 ½ teaspoons kosher salt
Canola or grapeseed oil
Unsalted butter if necessary
½ lemon

Preheat the oven to 450°F.

Season the fillets with the salt. Slick a large cast-iron skillet with oil and heat over medium-high heat. When you see a wisp of smoke, lay a fillet in the pan, skin side down, and immediately apply even pressure to it with a fish spatula if you have one, or whatever stiff spatula you have, pressing against the hot surface of the pan for 30 seconds. You might feel a subtle change as the flesh relaxes a little and stops resisting. At this point, you can release the pressure. Check the skin by gently lifting a corner of the fillet; if it needs a little more time to begin crisping, lower the heat and give it another 10 to 15 seconds. If you find that the skin sticks a little when you check on the crisping process, put a knob of butter in the pan and gently lift the corner of the fillet while tipping the pan so the butter flows under. The steam from the water in the butter should release the skin. When the first fillet is crisped, transfer it to a plate, skin side up, adjust the heat if necessary, and place the next fillet in the skillet to crisp. Repeat until the last fillet has crisped, then return all the fillets to the pan, skin side down.

Place the skillet on the floor of the oven and cook the fish according to its thickness—up to 8 minutes per inch. Use a metal skewer such as a cake tester (or a meat thermometer) to pierce the meat at its thickest point; when you remove the skewer, it should feel quite warm on your lip. If you are uncertain, flake off a piece from the portion you will serve yourself to check.

Serve with a squeeze of lemon over each fillet.

THE TIRELESS PEACE-MAKER, HE STRIVED TO BE BOTH FISH AND FOWL.

CRISPY-SKIN FISH FILLETS *with* GREEN GODDESS DRESSING

Braised lettuce, soft but with a trace of bite, adds another texture to this dish of crispy-skin fish, crunchy nuts, and my take on creamy green goddess dressing. I keep finding other ways to use this versatile dressing. My bet is you will too.

SERVES 4

Preheat the oven to 450°F.

MAKE THE GREEN GODDESS DRESSING

½ cup roughly chopped scallion greens

¼ cup watercress

¼ cup fresh herb leaves (such as flat-leaf parsley, chervil, tarragon, cilantro, and/or dill—singly or any mixture you have in the garden or fridge)

2 tablespoons mayonnaise

2 tablespoons sour cream

1 tablespoon water

2 anchovy fillets

Juice of ½ lemon

Put all the ingredients in a blender and run at high speed for about 30 seconds, until smooth.

BRAISE THE LETTUCE

Olive oil

3 heads Little Gem lettuce or romaine hearts, separated into leaves

Kosher salt

3 tablespoons Fish Fumet (page 98), chicken stock, or water

Slick a large skillet with oil and set over medium heat. Add the lettuce, give it a sprinkle of salt, and cook, turning occasionally, until wilted. Add the fumet or other liquid, lower the heat and cook a bit longer, about 3 minutes total. Remove to a platter and set aside.

MAKE THE CRISPY-SKIN FISH FILLETS (PAGE 104)

PUT IT ALL TOGETHER

Green Goddess Dressing

Braised lettuce

¼ cup fresh herb leaves (your choice)

Crispy-Skin Fish Fillets

⅓ cup hazelnuts or walnuts, toasted (page 17) and crushed

½ lemon

Spoon a puddle of the green goddess on a serving platter. Set some of the braised lettuce on the dressing, scatter some of the herbs over, and set the fillets on top. Scatter the remainder of the lettuces and herbs, along with the nuts, over and around the fish and drizzle the remaining green goddess here and there. Finish with an enthusiastic squeeze of lemon over each fillet.

CRISPY-SKIN FISH FILLETS *with* CASHEWS *in* BROWN BUTTER

Panfried fish in butter is a camp-fire stalwart. Often the brown butter is an unintended consequence, but a welcome one. Here I separate the butter browning from crisping the fish and unite them at the end. Cashews are little packages of savory buttery flavor with just the right amount of bite to match the texture of the fish.

SERVES 4

Preheat the oven to 450°F.

MAKE THE CASHEWS IN BROWN BUTTER

4 tablespoons (½ stick) unsalted butter
½ cup unsalted roasted cashews, roughly chopped
Grated zest of 1 lemon
Juice of ½ lemon
Kosher salt

Melt the butter in a small skillet over medium heat. Once the butter foams, add the cashews and continuously swirl the pan so that the butter browns evenly. You are looking for a golden brown color. Add the lemon zest, juice, and salt to taste. Pour into a bowl, brown bits and all.

MAKE THE CRISPY-SKIN FISH FILLETS (PAGE 104)

PUT IT ALL TOGETHER

Crispy-Skin Fish Fillets
Cashews in Brown Butter, rewarmed
½ brimming cup fresh mint leaves, with some tarragon and flat-leaf parsley leaves, chopped
½ lemon

Place the fillets on a serving plate or platter. Spoon the brown butter and cashews over the fish and scatter the herbs all over. Give each fillet a squeeze of lemon.

CRISPY-SKIN FISH FILLETS *with* FAVA MINT MASH

The first time I ate a fava mash was at the Boqueria, Barcelona's famous market, at a tiny lunch counter where two idiosyncratic and talented chefs cooked from the market offerings that day. Diners were waited on by a stern fellow in a tuxedo who dispensed cava by the gallon. It's first come, first served, and you score a seat at the bar by standing in line behind someone and waiting for them to finish and leave a seat for you. The kitchen sends out food in waves, and you are free to accept or not as the spirit moves you. After we sipped a little cava, the waiter asked if we'd like favas with anchovies. Of course we said yes, and out came a beautiful fava bean toast with two fat luscious anchovies, splashed with spectacular Spanish olive oil. I will be forever grateful to that *caballero* for introducing me to those favas. Here they are mashed with mint and olive oil, no anchovies. The mash has a gentle but distinct flavor and texture that is splendid with fish.

Note: *Pop the blanched fava beans out of their casings by using your thumb to pierce the skin. I find it helpful to set up a large bowl to catch the beans, since they can fly out of the skins at odd angles.*

SERVES 4

MAKE THE FAVA MINT MASH

3 cups shelled fava beans (from 3 to 4 pounds favas in the pod)

3 tablespoons olive oil plus 2 tablespoons oil from Oil-Poached Garlic or Shallots (page 20) or ⅓ cup olive oil

1 garlic clove, grated or minced

2 teaspoons kosher salt, or to taste

1 to 2 tablespoons Fish Fumet (page 98) or water

¼ cup fresh mint leaves

Bring a large pot of water to a boil. Set up an ice bath. Add the favas to the boiling water and blanch for 2 minutes, then drain and put in the ice bath. As soon as the beans have cooled, drain thoroughly and peel off the skin.

Combine the oil, garlic, salt, and 1 tablespoon of the fumet or water in a food processor and run until smooth; add up to 1 more tablespoon liquid if necessary. Add the favas and mint and pulse until the favas are half smooth and half chunky. You want the consistency to be like mashed potatoes, easily spreadable on a plate or platter. Check for seasoning.

MAKE THE CRISPY-SKIN FISH FILLETS (PAGE 104)

PUT IT ALL TOGETHER

Fava Mint Mash

Crispy-Skin Fish Fillets

½ lemon

Smear a platter with the fava mint mash, place the fish fillets on top, and squeeze some lemon juice on the fish. Serve it forth!

CRISPY-SKIN FISH FILLETS *with* SHELLFISH CHOWDER

What exactly is a chowder? There is no standard definition, though most people agree that it contains seafood plus some potato for body. This one is more 2020 than 1820, because I cook the various parts separately and bring them together at the end.

SERVES 4

MAKE THE CHOWDER BASE

1 tablespoon unsalted butter
1 tablespoon oil from Oil-Poached Shallots (page 20) or olive oil
2 medium shallots, thinly sliced
½ russet potato (you'll use the other half of the potato later), peeled and roughly chopped (about ½ cup)
1 pound celery root, peeled and chopped
1 celery stalk, cut into ¼-inch-thick slices
2 bay leaves
½ to 1 cup Fish Fumet (page 98) or white wine
1 cup heavy cream
Ground black pepper and kosher salt

Heat the butter and oil in a large saucepan over medium-high heat until hot. Add the shallots, potato, celery root, celery, and bay leaves and cook for 3 to 4 minutes, until the shallots are translucent. Add ½ cup of the fumet or white wine and cook for a minute or two (if using wine, this cooks off the alcohol). Add the cream and cook until the vegetables are soft, 15 to 20 minutes. Add more fumet, wine, or water to adjust the consistency. Season forcefully with black pepper and a healthy amount of salt.

Remove the bay leaves, transfer the base to a blender (it's important that you do this while the mixture is hot), and puree. Taste for consistency. Set aside.

COOK THE VEGETABLES AND SHELLFISH

Oil from Oil-Poached Shallots (page 20) or olive oil
½ cup roughly chopped peeled celery root
1 bay leaf
½ cup Fish Fumet (page 98) or white wine
½ russet potato, roughly chopped
2 medium shallots, thinly sliced
1 celery stalk, cut into ¼-inch-thick slices
8 littleneck clams, scrubbed
8 plump mussels, scrubbed and debearded if necessary

Heat the oil in a large skillet over medium-high heat. Add the celery root and bay leaf and sauté for 3 minutes. Add the fumet or wine and simmer for 5 minutes. Add the potato and shallots and cook, stirring from time to time, until the celery root is soft, about 10 minutes. Add some water if the pan starts to dry out. Add the celery and clams, cover, and cook for 2 minutes. Add the mussels, cover, and cook until they open—or at least smile. Remove the pan from the heat.

MAKE THE CRISPY-SKIN FISH FILLETS (PAGE 104)

PUT IT ALL TOGETHER

Chowder Base
Vegetables and shellfish
Crispy-Skin Fish Fillets

Rewarm the chowder base. If it seems too thick, dilute slightly with a little fumet or water.

Spoon the chowder base, some of the shellfish, and the vegetables into wide soup plates. Set the fish in the plates, wherever it looks best to you, and scatter the rest of the shellfish all around.

Gently Cooked Shrimp

GENTLY COOKED SHRIMP

BASIC RECIPE

I love the tender, juicy pop of a perfectly cooked shrimp. I've cooked them a thousand ways: seared in butter, skewered on the grill, blanched in boiling water and then shocked in ice. . . . The method here, a very low-temperature off-the-heat poach in a hot salty, sweet, and acidic liquid (a pared-down court bouillon) is simple and gentle, and it ensures success.

SERVES 4

4 cups water

¼ cup white vinegar, white wine vinegar, or cider vinegar

3 tablespoons kosher salt

3 tablespoons sugar

1 bay leaf

Zest from 1 lemon removed in strips with a vegetable peeler, plus the juice

1 pound medium (21 to 25 count) shrimp, peeled and deveined (save the shells for stock)

Combine the water, vinegar, salt, sugar, bay leaf, lemon zest, and lemon juice in a medium pot and bring to a boil, stirring until the salt and sugar dissolve. Turn off the heat and wait about 5 minutes, then add the shrimp. Stir gently and look for the shrimp to go from gray and translucent to pink and opaque, 4 to 5 minutes. Test a shrimp for doneness by slicing it in half and looking at the cross section: The middle of the shrimp should have just about tipped from translucent to white and opaque all the way through; even a little less is okay.

Scoop the shrimp onto a baking sheet or plate and leave them to cool, at room temperature or in the fridge.

POTTED SHRIMP

This is a dish that is often served in English pubs, made with a particular brown shrimp native to the British Isles. It is also diet-bustingly rich, but sublime. For the classic version, the shrimp are poached, but for a more delicate flavor, I prefer to cook mine the same gentle way I do in all of my shrimp recipes and then pot the cooked shrimps in the butter. The Brits customarily serve it in ramekins with a few saltines alongside—a delightfully unfussy touch. Serve with Leafy Salad (page 214).

SERVES 4 TO 8 AS AN APPETIZER

MAKE THE GENTLY COOKED SHRIMP (OPPOSITE); SAVE THE SHELLS

When the shrimp are cooked, let cool, then refrigerate.

MAKE THE SHRIMP-SHELL BUTTER

Reserved shrimp shells
¼ cup dry sherry, plus a splash
½ pound (2 sticks) unsalted butter, softened
½ teaspoon spicy paprika
¼ teaspoon ground nutmeg
½ teaspoon kosher salt

Preheat the oven to 450°F.

Put the shells in an ovenproof skillet and roast in the oven for about 8 minutes, until they are bright pink but not yet browned. Remove the skillet from the oven (the handle will be hot!) and place over high heat, then add the sherry. The shells will absorb the sherry quickly, but it will take a minute or two to cook off the alcohol. Dump the shells into the bowl of a food processor and pulverize, scraping down the sides as needed. This will take a few scrapings and a few minutes—you want the shells super broken up.

Combine the shells with the softened butter, paprika, nutmeg, and salt in the bowl of a standing mixer fitted with the paddle attachment and beat until the mixture turns uniformly pink, at least 3 minutes. Scrape down the bowl 3 or 4 times.

Using the back of a large metal spoon, push about a third of the mixture at a time through a sieve into a bowl for delightfully pink butter infused with the flavors of shrimp shells (it's easier when you do this in batches).

CONTINUED

MAKE THE POTTED SHRIMP

Gently Cooked Shrimp
Shrimp-Shell Butter

Pulse the shrimp in a food processor until the consistency of picked crab. Transfer to a medium bowl. Add the butter to the bowl and mix with the shrimp using a rubber spatula or large wooden spoon. Divide the shrimp among four 4-ounce (or eight 2-ounce) ramekins, cover, and refrigerate for a day, so the flavors have some time to meld.

PUT IT ALL TOGETHER

Potted Shrimp
Saltines or toast
4 to 8 lemon wedges

A half hour before serving, take the ramekins out of the refrigerator and let them stand at room temperature. Serve with saltines or toast and the lemon wedges.

"Actually, Je préfèr
to be called a
'2.54 cm' Worm"

SHRIMP SALAD *with* PEAS *(or Celery)*, DILL, *and* TARRAGON

This recipe is pretty faithful to the shrimp salad that my friend Charlie does at his market shop on the East End of Long Island. What's so special about Charlie and his shrimp is a lesson that all cooks would do well to remember: You can do a lot with just a few ingredients if the ingredients are great and you do it well. If you don't have a Charlie in your life, here's an at-home version that will serve you well for a cool supper on a hot night. Use the best-quality cream you can get your hands on. If there is a dairy farmer at your local farmers' market, go for it. If you can't get great fresh peas, raw celery is a fine alternative; indeed, it's what Charlie always uses.

SERVES 4

MAKE THE GENTLY COOKED SHRIMP (PAGE 114)

COOK THE PEAS

1 brimming cup green peas, or 2 celery stalks, thinly sliced

If using peas, bring 2 quarts of water to a boil in a large saucepan and blanch the peas for 2 to 3 minutes. They should soften but not become wrinkly or mushy. Drain in a colander and cool them under cold running water. If using celery, leave it raw.

MAKE THE SHRIMP SALAD

Gently Cooked Shrimp
Cooked peas or celery
2 small or 1 large scallion, thinly sliced
⅓ brimming cup fresh dill leaves, chopped
1¼ cups heavy cream
Kosher salt

Put the shrimp, peas or celery, scallions, dill, and cream in a medium bowl and mix well. There's no spice or acidity for salt to play against, so add it with a light hand. You can serve the salad right away or rest it in the fridge for a day or two. Resting allows the cream to meld the flavors of all the ingredients.

PUT IT ALL TOGETHER

½ cup mixed fresh soft herbs (I like tarragon, chervil, cilantro, parsley, and dill)
1 to 2 handfuls leaves from Little Gem lettuce or romaine hearts
Olive oil
White wine vinegar
Kosher salt
Shrimp Salad

Toss the herbs with the lettuce in a bowl and lightly dress with oil, vinegar, and salt. Put the dressed lettuce and herbs on a platter. Spoon the shrimp salad on top, making sure that you get all the flavorful cream.

SPICY SHRIMP, PEANUTS, CILANTRO, *and* MINT

I love Thai food: its spiciness, its sweetness, its profligate use of herbs, that funky fishy smell. I wanted to re-create the flavor profile of a Thai recipe with Western ingredients. I think this is a good example of how different food cultures can arrive at similar dishes, because the human animal, no matter where, tends to like the same basic flavors.

SERVES 4

MAKE THE GENTLY COOKED SHRIMP (PAGE 114)

MAKE THE HOT SAUCE

2 anchovy fillets, plus 1 tablespoon of the oil they are packed in
3 tablespoons olive oil
2 tablespoons fresh lemon juice, or to taste
1 tablespoon white wine vinegar
2 teaspoons honey
1 ¼ teaspoons crushed red pepper flakes, or to taste
¼ teaspoon kosher salt, or to taste

Chop and mash the anchovy fillets into a paste, then transfer to a bowl and whisk together with the anchovy oil, olive oil, lemon juice, vinegar, honey, cayenne, and salt.

ASSEMBLE THE SPICY SHRIMP SALAD

Gently Cooked Shrimp
½ cup crushed roasted peanuts
1 cup mixed fresh cilantro and mint leaves, chopped
Hot Sauce

Mix the shrimp with the peanuts, cilantro and mint, and hot sauce in a large bowl, giving it all a good stir. Check for seasoning and acidity and adjust if necessary.

PUT IT ALL TOGETHER

Spicy Shrimp Salad
½ teaspoon ground coriander
½ lime

Put the shrimp on individual plates or serve family-style in a bowl. Dust with the coriander and serve with the lime.

LOBSTER-STYLE SHRIMP ROLLS

This recipe was inspired by the dockside lobster rolls that are as much a Maine tradition as the Stars and Stripes are at a town parade on July 4th. Sour cream and lemon brighten the mayo. I recommend top-sliced hot dog rolls because the salad tends to fall out of a roll that is sliced completely into two. But stuff each roll to overflowing, because a shrimp roll that doesn't overflow is an affront to decency.

MAKES 4 ROLLS

MAKE THE GENTLY COOKED SHRIMP (PAGE 114)

MAKE THE SHRIMP SALAD

Gently Cooked Shrimp
1/4 cup mayonnaise, preferably homemade (page 21)
1/4 cup sour cream
2 celery stalks, halved lengthwise and thinly sliced
1 tablespoon chopped fresh tarragon
Grated zest and juice of 1/2 lemon, or more juice to taste
1/2 teaspoon kosher salt, or to taste
Dash of spicy paprika (optional)

Chop the shrimp into small bite-sized chunks. Mix the shrimp together with the mayonnaise, sour cream, celery, tarragon, lemon zest and juice, salt, and paprika, if using, in a bowl, giving them a good stir. Loosen just a bit with water if needed. Taste for salt, spiciness, and tanginess.

PUT IT ALL TOGETHER

4 top-sliced hot dog rolls
2 teaspoons melted unsalted butter
Shrimp Salad
Paprika

Toast the buns in a hot oven or a toaster oven. Brush the insides with the butter, then fill with the shrimp salad. Dust each roll with a dash of paprika.

CURRY-SAUCE SHRIMP ROLLS

Curry pairs fabulously with shellfish. In this homemade curry mayo, it amplifies the shrimpness.

MAKES 4 ROLLS

MAKE THE GENTLY COOKED SHRIMP (PAGE 114); SAVE THE SHELLS

When the shrimp are done, preheat the oven to 500°F so that you can put everything together as soon as you finish making the sauce and mayonnaise.

MAKE THE CURRY SAUCE

1 tablespoon oil from Oil-Poached Garlic or Shallots (page 20) or canola or grapeseed oil
Reserved shrimp shells
1 medium onion, thinly sliced
3 celery stalks, halved lengthwise and thinly sliced
1 ½ tablespoons curry powder
Cayenne pepper
2 teaspoons tomato paste
1 cup white wine

Heat the oil in a large saucepan over high heat. When you see the first wisp of smoke, add the shrimp shells. Cook until the shells turn pinkish and even a touch brown here and there, just a minute or two. Add the onion, celery, curry, and cayenne to taste and cook for 3 minutes, stirring frequently. Add the tomato paste and cook for another 2 minutes, then add the wine. Cook for 3 minutes, or until the pan is almost but not quite dry. Add just enough water to cover the shells and bring to a boil, then immediately reduce the heat to a faint simmer and set a timer for 15 minutes.

When the timer goes off, strain the sauce into a small saucepan (discard the solids) and reduce to about ¼ cup. Take care that it doesn't scorch or burn as it reduces. Set aside to cool.

MAKE THE CURRY MAYONNAISE

Curry Sauce
1 large egg yolk
1 tablespoon minced ginger
Grated zest and juice of 1 lime
¼ to ½ teaspoon kosher salt (to taste)
1 cup canola or grapeseed oil

Combine the curry sauce, egg yolk, ginger, lime zest and juice, and salt in a food processor and run for 10 to 15 seconds. Check to see that everything has combined. There will still be some flecks of ginger; don't worry, that's fine. With the food processor running, drizzle in some of the oil in a thin stream for 15 to 20 seconds, then add the remaining oil in a slightly thicker stream, processing for 30 to 45 seconds, until the mixture is just about as thick as Hellmann's mayonnaise.

MAKE THE SHRIMP SALAD

Gently Cooked Shrimp
Curry Mayonnaise

Cut the shrimp into small bite-sized chunks. Combine the shrimp and mayonnaise in a bowl. Taste for salt, spice, and acidity and adjust to taste.

PUT IT ALL TOGETHER

4 top-sliced hot dog rolls
2 teaspoons melted unsalted butter
Shrimp Salad
2 scallions, very thinly sliced, and/or ⅓ cup fresh cilantro leaves or your favorite herbs, chopped

Toast the rolls in a hot oven or a toaster oven. Brush on the butter and fill the rolls with the shrimp salad. Garnish with the scallions and/or cilantro or other herbs.

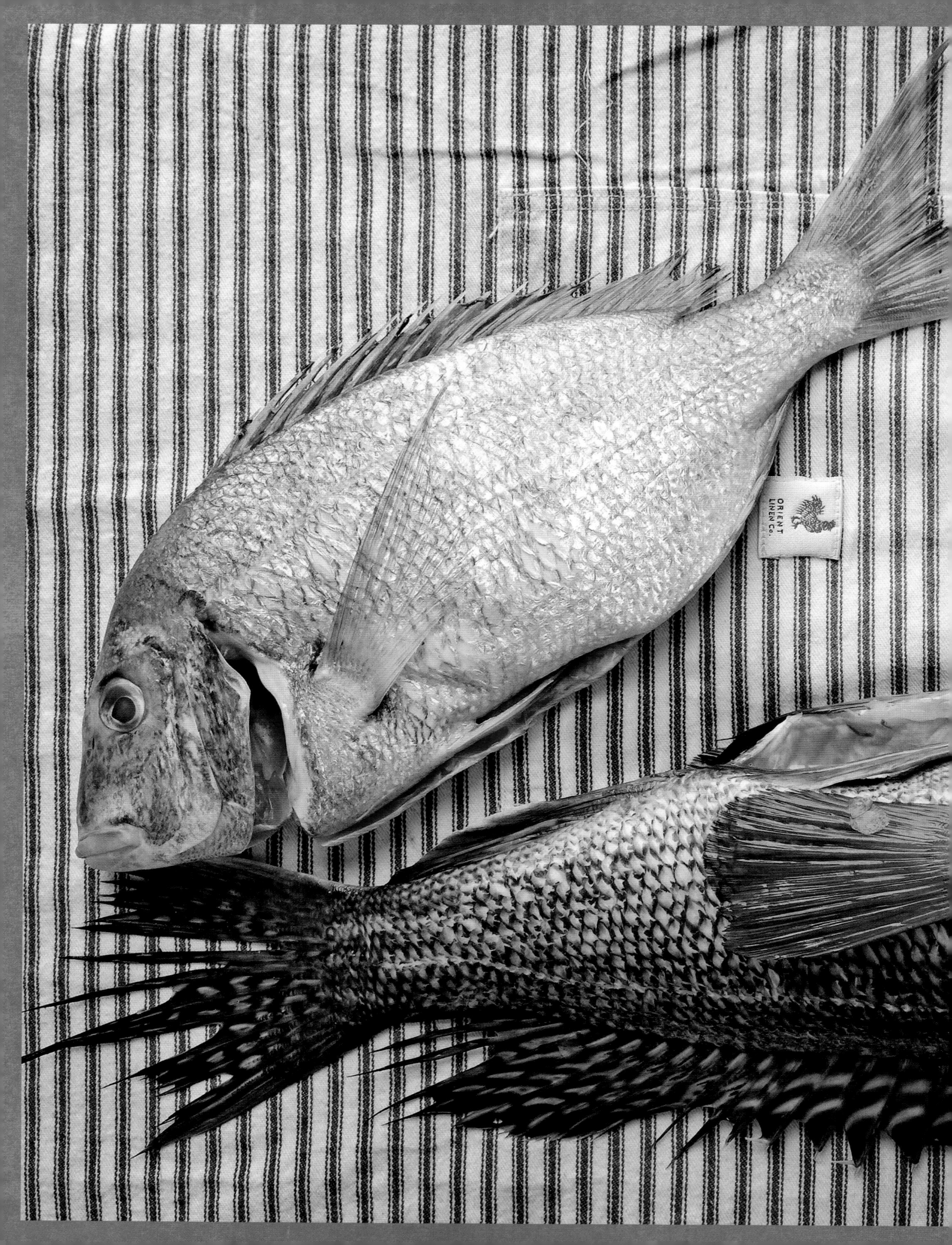
ORIENT
LINEN Co.

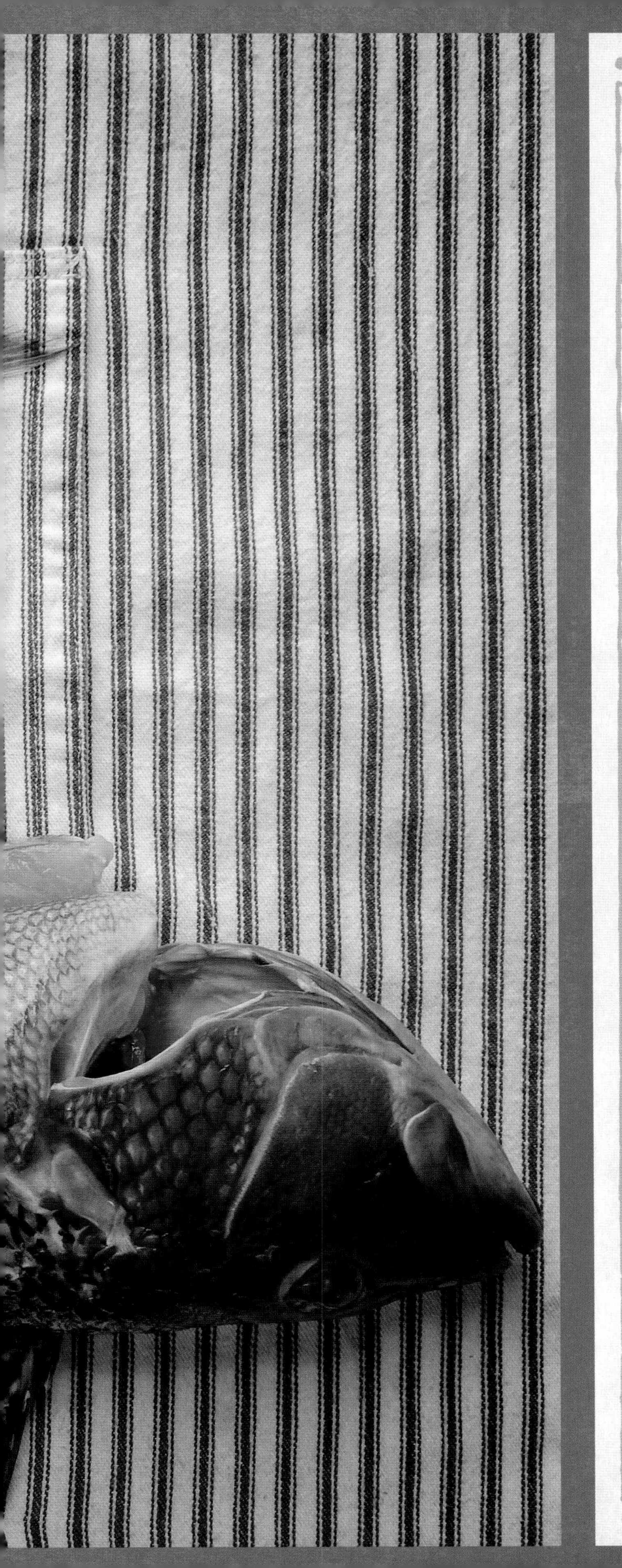

GRILLED WHOLE SEA BASS (OR OTHER FISH)

GRILLED WHOLE SEA BASS
(or Other Fish)

BASIC RECIPE

Although Americans are among the grillingest of nations, many backyard barbecuers shy away from grilling a whole fish. This is too bad because fish prepared in this ancient style is supremely flavorful and handsome: stuffed with fragrant herbs and perhaps a slice of lemon, with slashes of char. What holds many good grillers back is the fear that the skin will stick to the grill. You're not a failure if some of the skin sticks to the grill. For some reason, people imagine that "real chefs" never let the skin stick. They do. I have.

I learned a lot about grilling whole fish working in a restaurant where I cooked fifteen to twenty fish every night. A clean oiled grill, oiled fish, and a careful and resolute two-handed flip of the fish will yield juicy well-cooked flesh and crispy skin . . . nearly every time.

I am partial to black sea bass, which is quite plentiful in our local waters and not overfished. Other fish that are well suited to grilling are red snapper, porgy, Spanish mackerel, small bluefish, and blackfish (aka tautog). Freshwater anglers can try bass (smallmouth and largemouth), walleye, big crappie, or bluegill.

SERVES 4

PREP THE FISH AND HEAT THE GRILL

2 fish (see headnote), 1 to 1½ pounds each
2 to 3 tablespoons oil from Oil-Poached Garlic or Shallots (page 20) or canola or grapeseed oil
1 teaspoon kosher salt

Rub the fish evenly all over with oil (don't drench it). Sprinkle the salt all over.

Give the grill bars a good scrub with a metal brush, then wipe them down with an oiled rag. (A grill with a thicker grate works better than the classic Weber, but you can work with whatever you have.) Fire up the grill; you want medium-high heat. Temperate, even heat is the goal. Too hot, and you'll lose control. You'll need a pair of tongs as well as a metal spatula.

GRILL THE FISH

Olive oil for drizzling
Lemon or lime wedges

Find a spot on the grill with fairly even heat and gently lay the fish down there. The heads should go over the hotter part of the grill so the thickest meat gets the most heat. Once you put fish on the grill, leave it, even if it's not exactly in the prime spot. After 4 minutes, use your fish spatula to gently lift up part of each fish to see if the skin is sticking and if you've established a crust. If there's no crust yet, leave it for another minute or two. If the fish isn't sticking, reach over and put your spatula in the organ cavity of each fish and roll it over. This is an effective movement if your goal is to touch the fish as little as possible. If you are not sure about this maneuver, gently insert the spatula under the fish while pulling it up by the head with a pair of tongs. Even if it sticks a little, turn the fish over and leave it alone to finish cooking. After another 4 or 5 minutes, use a metal skewer such as a cake tester or a meat thermometer to pierce the meat at its thickest point. When you remove the skewer, it should feel quite warm on your lip. If it is, you can remove the fish from the grill. If you're really not sure, fleck a bit off the part that you will serve yourself.

Wielding your tongs in one hand and the spatula in the other, use the tongs to lift the head, slide the spatula under the body, and lift the fish off the grill and onto a serving plate. Drizzle some oil all over and garnish with lemon or lime.

CLEANING FISH (AND SAVING THE FISH YOU LOVE)

Whatever fish I cook, I want to know that I am sourcing it from environmentally responsible suppliers. I much prefer to stay with sustainably harvested wild fish. The Monterey Bay Aquarium has an app that is very helpful (seafoodwatch.org/seafood-recommendations/our-app_); so does the Safina Center (safinacenter.org/files/Seafood_Guide.pdf).

I leave the head and the tail on; it's a better look. If the fishmonger has not done so, remove the scales and gills and clean out the belly. You might snip off the pectoral fins that extend just behind the gills. Fish blood is where a lot of off-putting "fishy" taste comes from, so make sure you give the fish a thorough rinse under cold running water. Afterward, it's critical to dry the fish well inside and out. You can do this with paper towels or by leaving it uncovered on a rack in the fridge for a couple of hours.

BLACK SEA BASS *with* SCORCHED ENDIVE *and a* BIG VINAIGRETTE

Endives and their close botanical cousins in the chicory family (especially Treviso and common red radicchio) are ideally suited to scorching, creating a stiletto stab of bitter and burnt that wakes up the palate. Your aim is not so much to cook the endive as it is to create some char. Any sturdy-leafed vegetable, especially with a burnt part here and there, can stand up to a robust vinaigrette.

Note: *Although you can stuff the fish right before cooking, if you do it the day before, the fragrance of the tarragon and lemon will infuse the flesh.*

SERVES 4

PREP THE FISH AND HEAT THE GRILL

Oil and salt the fish and heat the grill as directed on page 126.

STUFF THE FISH

2 small lemons (one per fish), thinly sliced into rounds
1 bunch fresh tarragon
A few pinches of kosher salt

Stuff the fish cavities with the lemon slices. Cram the tarragon into the heads, stem ends first, to lodge them securely. (The fish can be refrigerated overnight before grilling, if desired; see Note above.)

SCORCH THE ENDIVE

2 large or 3 medium endive

Cut each endive lengthwise in half; leave the root ends to hold the leaves together. When the fire is really hot, put the endive cut side down on the grate for no more than a minute, maybe less. Set aside on a plate.

MAKE THE VINAIGRETTE

1 garlic clove, peeled
4 anchovy fillets
1 to 2 teaspoons capers, drained
Pinch of cayenne pepper
Grated zest and juice of 1 lemon
¾ cup Herb-Infused Oil (page 20) or olive oil
Kosher salt

You can make this vinaigrette in a blender or food processor. Combine all the ingredients except the salt and run for about 30 seconds. Taste the dressing before salting because the anchovies are good and salty, then add a pinch of salt if needed.

GRILL THE FISH

Grill the fish as directed on page 126.

PUT IT ALL TOGETHER

Grilled Whole Black Sea Bass
Scorched Endive
Vinaigrette
4 lemon cheeks (page 163)

Arrange the fish and endive on a platter however you like. Give the dressing a stir and spoon over the endive, and get some on the fish too. Serve with the lemon cheeks.

BLACK SEA BASS *with* POTATOES *and* NUTTY GREEN SAUCE

Cooking the potatoes on the grill infuses them with the appealing, rustic flavor of the smoke. The herbal sauce feels of the season, and then there's the pleasing buttery crunch you always get with nuts.

SERVES 4

COOK THE POTATOES

1 ½ pounds new potatoes
2 garlic cloves, thinly sliced
1 small shallot, thinly sliced
4 sprigs of fresh thyme
½ teaspoon kosher salt
¼ cup oil from Oil-Poached Garlic or Shallots (page 20) or olive oil
2 tablespoons water

Fire up the grill: You want a medium-hot fire.

Cut the potatoes into large bite-sized pieces, probably halves or quarters. Tear off two 12-inch squares of foil. Divide the potatoes between them and fold up the edges of each square to form a lip. Scatter the garlic, shallot, and thyme over the potatoes, sprinkle with the salt, and drizzle the oil and water over them. Bring the edges of the foil up over the potatoes and seal tightly.

Set the pouches away from direct flame on the grill and close the lid. Cook for 20 minutes, or until the potatoes are soft.

MEANWHILE, MAKE THE NUTTY GREEN SAUCE

½ cup whole almonds, crushed
1 cup canola or grapeseed oil
4 scallions
1 cup fresh flat-leaf parsley leaves, minced
½ cup fresh mint leaves, minced
¼ cup fresh tarragon leaves, minced
⅛ teaspoon crushed red pepper flakes
Grated zest of 1 lemon

Combine the almonds and oil in a small saucepan and cook over medium heat, stirring frequently, until the nuts smell toasty, 4 to 7 minutes. Drain the nuts in a strainer, then spread on a paper towel to cool. Let the oil cool. You're going to use it too.

Cut the green tops from the scallions and reserve. Place the white parts of the scallions crosswise on the grill rack and, grill until they're soft all the way through. Remove from the grill.

When the scallions have cooled, chop them and put them in a bowl. Mince the raw green tops and add to the bowl. Add the herbs, the cooled almonds, red pepper, lemon zest, and the oil the almonds were cooked in. Give it all a good stir to combine.

PREP THE FISH

Oil and salt the fish as directed on page 126.

STUFF THE FISH

1 small lemon, cut into ¼-inch-thick slices
A handful of fresh flat-leaf parsley and tarragon sprigs

Stuff the fish cavities with the slices of lemon. Cram the herbs into the heads, stem end first, to lodge them securely.

GRILL THE FISH

Grill the fish as directed on page 126. Transfer to a platter.

PUT IT ALL TOGETHER

Potatoes
Grilled Whole Black Sea Bass
Nutty Green Sauce
1 teaspoon flaky salt
4 fat lemon cheeks (page 163)

Place the potatoes alongside the fish on a platter. Spoon the sauce wherever you like. Sprinkle the salt all over and serve with the lemon cheeks.

BLACK SEA BASS *with* SPICED ORANGE SLICES *and* WARM SLAW

Slaw is a time-honored partner for grilled fish. Here grilled orange slices brighten the slaw and echo the oranges in the stuffing for the sea bass. I have served this slaw with roast chicken and pot-roasted pork. It's a keeper.

You can stuff the fish ahead and refrigerate it for as long as 24 hours so the flavor of the spices and orange infuse the flesh.

Note: *Urfa is a mildly spicy Turkish pepper. Urfa pepper flakes are available in Middle Eastern markets and online.*

SERVES 4

PREP THE FISH AND HEAT THE GRILL

Oil and salt the fish and heat the grill as directed on page 126.

STUFF THE FISH

2 oranges, sliced into ¼-inch-thick rounds or half-moons
Kosher salt
Aleppo pepper, Urfa pepper, or spicy paprika
Urfa pepper to taste
A handful of fresh thyme sprigs

Lay the orange slices on a cutting board and sprinkle lightly with salt and the pepper or paprika. Stuff each fish with 3 or 4 orange slices. (You'll have lots of orange slices left over; reserve them.) Stuff the thyme stem ends first, into the head cavity. Set aside, or refrigerate for up to 24 hours.

MAKE THE WARM SLAW

⅛ medium head green cabbage
¼ cup oil from Oil-Poached Garlic or Shallots (page 20) or olive oil
1 medium-large red onion, thinly sliced
6 sprigs of fresh thyme
⅓ cup julienned (matchsticks) peeled ginger
1 teaspoon kosher salt
A little minced serrano chili (how much is your call)

Remove the cabbage core and slice the rest crosswise into ribbons about ½ inch wide.

Heat the oil in a deep pot over high heat. Add the onion and thyme and cook for 60 seconds. Add the cabbage, ginger, and salt and cook, stirring, until the cabbage is shiny, its green color has intensified, and the texture has relaxed a little but it still retains lots of crunch, about 5 minutes. Set aside in a bowl.

GRILL THE FISH

Grill the fish as directed on page 126. Transfer to a platter.

MEANWHILE, FINISH THE SLAW

Reserved orange slices
Warm Slaw
Juice of 1 lemon
Aleppo pepper, Urfa pepper, or spicy paprika

Grill the reserved orange slices for a minute or so. If they blacken in spots, you're doing it right. Transfer the oranges to a bowl and add the slaw, lemon juice, and a liberal amount of pepper or paprika.

PUT IT ALL TOGETHER

Warm Slaw
Grilled Whole Black Sea Bass
Olive oil

Spread the slaw out on a platter. Lay the fish on top and Finish with a drizzle of the olive oil.

BLACK SEA BASS *with* CHARRED CHERRIES *and* PEPPERS

Cherry season aligns with the time of year when colorful sweet peppers appear in farm stands. The grilled peppers and cherries are also wonderful with fish fillets and roast chicken.

SERVES 4

PREP THE FISH AND HEAT THE GRILL

Oil and salt the fish and heat the grill as described on page 126.

CHAR THE PEPPERS AND CHERRIES

3 or 4 yellow or red bell peppers, or a mix
24 Rainier or other sweet cherries
3 tablespoons olive oil
2 tablespoons white wine vinegar
1 to 2 tablespoons chopped fresh thyme, oregano, or marjoram
½ teaspoon kosher salt
½ teaspoon crushed red pepper flakes, or to taste

Place the peppers on the hottest part of the grill and grill, turning them every minute or so, until charred all over. The exact timing depends on the temperature of the grill, but it will likely be between 5 and 10 minutes. Transfer the peppers to a container with a lid, or put them in a bowl and set a plate on top, to steam and cool.

When the peppers are cool enough to handle, peel off the charred skins, then cut in half and remove the cores and seeds. Slice lengthwise into ½-inch-wide strips and put in a bowl.

Place the cherries on the grill; if the cherries are likely to fall through grill grate, use a grilling basket or, failing that, a skillet. When the cherries begin to char and weep, remove them and let cool.

When you can handle the cherries, roughly cut them in half and remove the pits; don't be fussy about the cutting. Add them to the bowl with the sliced peppers and then add the oil, vinegar, herbs, salt, and crushed red pepper. Set aside to marinate.

STUFF AND GRILL THE FISH

1 bunch fresh thyme, oregano, or marjoram (whatever you chose for charred pepper and cherries)

Cram the herbs into the head, stem ends first, to lodge them securely. Grill the fish as directed on page 126.

PUT IT ALL TOGETHER

Grilled Whole Black Sea Bass
Charred Peppers and Cherries

Lay the fish on a platter and spread the pepper-cherry mix over it.

Broccoli

ROASTED BROCCOLI

BASIC RECIPE

I'm glad to live in an age when broccoli has gone from a punch line to a star in the theater of vegetables. It accepts many other flavorings: spices, herbs, nuts, capers, anchovies.

How long you cook broccoli depends on how you like it. I'm partial to broccoli with a little snap, and my kids will have it no other way. Some people, though, like a softer vegetable, and others like theirs very crunchy. Peter searches out the brown roasty parts. Happily, a properly roasted piece of broccoli has it all, from glistening bright green and crisp to brown or even a little black. Well-salted and with a squeeze of lemon, it makes for a simple, satisfying plate. I do cook all of the recipes in this chapter at home, but truthfully, more often than not, I just make this basic version. My kids love it.

SERVES 4

PREP THE BROCCOLI

2 broccoli heads

Preheat the oven to 400°F.

Because of the architecture of broccoli, some simple swipes of a knife will break it down into some elaborate-looking rococo pieces. Follow the floret to where it attaches to the main stem and snap it off the way a windstorm does the branches of a large tree. Work your way through both heads in this fashion, until you're left with a pile of wispy-ended stemmed florets. Peel each stem until you get to the slightly translucent core, then slice that up however you want and add the pieces to the pile.

COOK THE BROCCOLI

2 to 3 tablespoons canola or grapeseed oil
Kosher salt
Juice of 1 lemon

Pour the oil into a large (13-inch) ovenproof skillet (or use two 9-inch skillets) and heat over high heat for 30 to 60 seconds. Add the broccoli, salt liberally, and toss to coat with oil. Reduce the heat to medium-high and cook the broccoli for 4 to 5 minutes, turning once. The florets should start to develop some caramelized patches.

Put the pan(s) in the oven and roast for 6 to 8 minutes. When you taste for doneness, the stems should still have a little snap to them while the florets will be softer. Put the broccoli on a plate or baking sheet lined with paper towels to drain briefly.

PUT IT ALL TOGETHER

Broccoli
Olive oil
Kosher salt
Fresh lemon juice

Dress the broccoli with a little oil, some salt, and lemon juice and serve.

BROCCOLI *with* PICKLED GOLDEN RAISINS *and* TOASTED SUNFLOWER SEEDS

Sweet, sour, salty, crunchy, toasty, nutty: This is one of my greatest hits. This dish can be served hot, tepid, or cold. I'm happy to eat it at any temperature.

SERVES 4

MAKE THE ROASTED BROCCOLI (PAGE 138)

MEANWHILE, MAKE THE PICKLED RAISINS

2 tablespoons sugar
1 tablespoon kosher salt
1 teaspoon crushed red pepper flakes
½ cup white wine vinegar
½ cup water
½ cup sultana (golden) raisins

Combine the sugar, salt, red pepper flakes, vinegar, water, and raisins in a small saucepan set over medium-high heat. Bring to a boil, turn the heat off, and leave to steep for at least 10 minutes. Drain, reserving some of the liquid.

PUT IT ALL TOGETHER

Roasted Broccoli
½ cup sunflower seeds, toasted (page 17)
1 brimming cup fresh mint leaves, chopped
Pickled Raisins, plus 2 tablespoons of the cooking liquid
2 tablespoons fresh lemon juice
Kosher salt to taste

When the broccoli is cool enough to handle, transfer it to a bowl, add the remaining ingredients, and mix.

BROCCOLI *with* POACHED PRUNES *and* SPECK *(or Prosciutto)*

Although it's hard to beat the time-honored pairing of melon and prosciutto in the summertime, when the harvest is done and delicate green vegetables have signed off until another season is when I go for this plate with warm plumped prunes, broccoli, and sliced speck (smoked prosciutto). Or substitute regular prosciutto or even thinly sliced country ham. It's a combination that goes long on assertive tastes and textures.

SERVES 4

MAKE THE BROCCOLI

1 broccoli head
1 to 2 tablespoons canola oil
Kosher salt

Prep the broccoli as directed on page 138, but slice the florets lengthwise in half.

Cook the broccoli as directed in the basic recipe, but use a 9-inch skillet. Set aside in a bowl.

POACH THE PRUNES

10 prunes, pitted and quartered
About ½ cup red wine vinegar (enough to cover the prunes)

Put the prunes in a small saucepan, add the red wine vinegar, and simmer for 15 to 20 minutes. Drain the prunes in a strainer set over a small bowl; reserve the vinegar.

PUT IT ALL TOGETHER

Broccoli
Reserved vinegar (from the prunes)
½ cup soft goat cheese
A few tablespoons or so of heavy cream
Poached prunes
¼ pound sliced speck or prosciutto (or thinly sliced country ham)
½ cup hazelnuts, toasted (page 17)
A few drizzles of olive oil (optional)
Flaky sea salt

Toss the broccoli with 1 to 2 tablespoons of the vinegar. Save the rest of the vinegar for a sweet-and-tart salad dressing.

Put the cheese in a bowl and loosen with the cream until it's the consistency of ricotta. Place dollops of cheese on a serving plate. Scatter the broccoli around the plate, and then the prunes. Drape the speck or prosciutto over the broccoli. Scatter the hazelnuts all over. Finish with a drizzle of oil, if you like, sprinkle with flaky salt, and serve.

As a self-made man, Sal
owed a lot to duct tape.

BROCCOLI *and* FRIED CHICKPEAS *with* DUKKAH SPICE

A chickpea can have no higher calling on this earth than being fried and coated in the Egyptian nut and spice mix called *dukkah*. No doubt you're going to want to start snacking on the spiced chickpeas by themselves. Don't deny yourself; you might even make twice as much as called for here. Unless you have dried chickpeas in the pantry and feel like cooking them, use canned ones. They fry up great.

SERVES 4

MAKE THE ROASTED BROCCOLI (PAGE 138)

MAKE THE FRIED CHICKPEAS

1 ½ cups canned chickpeas, rinsed and thoroughly drained

2 cups canola or grapeseed oil

2 to 3 tablespoons homemade Dukkah, (page 39) or store-bought

½ teaspoon kosher salt, or more to taste

To make sure they don't spatter when you put them in the hot oil, pat the chickpeas dry on paper towels. Heat the oil in a small deep saucepan to 350°F. For safety, make sure that the oil comes no more than one third of the way up the sides of the saucepan (a good rule of thumb for frying anything on the stove), because the hot oil will bubble up vigorously when you add the chickpeas.

Add the chickpeas to the hot oil and fry for 4 to 5 minutes, until they turn a deep golden color. Drain them in a strainer set over a bowl. Immediately transfer the warm chickpeas to another bowl and toss with the dukkah spice until coated. The heat of the chickpeas will "bloom" the flavors of the spice mix. Sprinkle with the salt and set aside on a plate or paper towel.

MAKE THE DRESSING

1 shallot, minced

1 jalapeño, minced (include the seeds if you want the heat)

1 teaspoon minced ginger

2 tablespoons fresh lemon juice

2 tablespoons olive oil, or more if needed

1 teaspoon honey

½ teaspoon kosher salt

Put the ingredients in a bowl and mix well. If the dressing needs a little more oil, add it.

PUT IT ALL TOGETHER

1 cup Greek-style yogurt or labneh

Roasted Broccoli

Grated zest of ½ lemon

2 tablespoons fresh oregano

Fried Chickpeas

Dressing

Kosher salt

Smear the yogurt or labneh on a platter. Set the broccoli on the platter and sprinkle the lemon zest over it. Scatter on the oregano, followed by the chickpeas. You probably won't need them all; save the extra for snacks. Drizzle the dressing all over, check for salt, and serve.

Pot-Roasted Beets

POT-ROASTED BEETS

BASIC RECIPE

There are some things about us that get better as we age. An enjoyment of beets is one of them. While picky youngsters have been known turn up their noses, adults, just as reliably, come back for seconds. For reasons of deep food science (beets are alkaline and pickle brine is acidic) beets are ideal pickling candidates, which is no doubt why so many beet recipes call for boiling them in vinegared water. I prefer to pot-roast them in a tightly sealed environment—a Dutch oven covered with foil and then the lid. I don't even season the beets before cooking. As they steam, the juices that escape the beets are trapped in the cooking chamber and remain for you to use to intensify the beetiness. When they are done, I toss the beets with a little red vinegar, some olive oil, and a few pinches of salt, along with those juices.

Note: *Although folks tend to cook beets in the colder months, beets freshly dug in the summer are spectacular in the way that fresh-from-the-garden vegetables always are.*

SERVES 4

1 pound beets
Kosher salt
1 tablespoon red wine vinegar, or to taste
A few glugs of olive oil

Preheat the oven to 300°F.

Wash the beets. Leave the root ends on and trim the stems to about ½ inch. Put them in a Dutch oven or other heavy pot with a lid. Cover the pot with foil and then put the lid on top. Although it is obvious, I'll go ahead and say it anyway: *Beets the size of a baseball will take longer to cook than beets the size of a golf ball.* You never really know what size beet you're going to find at the market, and farmers often include beets of varying sizes in one bunch.

Put the beets in the oven. If they are golf ball–sized, check them after 45 minutes; if they are larger, check after 75 minutes. Important: When you check the beets, roll them over, because they could scorch on the hot bottom if you don't turn them. You'll know that they're done if when you insert a thin knife into the center of a beet, it slides in without any resistance. Remove the beets from the oven and let them cool somewhat, until you can handle them.

I find that beets are easiest to peel when they are still warm. Peel them by holding each one in your palm and rubbing the skin away with your thumb. If you don't want to get your hands all beety, use wadded-up paper towels (or a sacrificial dish towel dedicated hereafter to beets) and rub the beets roughly with the towel. Break up the beets with your hands into largeish bite-sized pieces, creating arroyos and canyons that will trap a flavorful vinaigrette. Transfer to a bowl.

If you kept a tight seal on the pot, the beets will have rendered some liquid. Pour the liquid through a sieve onto the beets. Sprinkle with some salt, add the red wine vinegar, and pour some olive oil all over them. Toss gently with a spoon and refrigerate in a sealed container, where they will marinate nicely until ready to use.

BEETS *with* ENDIVE *and* ORANGE

The flavors of this combination are strong, so you want robust leafy vegetables like endive or radicchio. I particularly like this with toasted pistachios. If you don't have pistachios on hand, almonds or hazelnuts are fine. You can certainly start from scratch, toasting the nuts in the oil and using that oil (see page 17), but part of the beauty of this (and many another) recipe is how having things ready to rock in your pantry makes for speedier recipes and less washing of plates and pots and pans. If you do make the nuts and oil from scratch, give the oil time to cool before using it in the dressing.

SERVES 4

MAKE THE POT-ROASTED BEETS (OPPOSITE)

Cook the beets, peel, and break them up as directed opposite; put the beets and any liquid the beets have given up in a medium bowl.

MAKE THE VINAIGRETTE

½ cup pistachio-, almond-, or hazelnut-infused oil (see Toasted Seeds and Nuts, page 17)
Grated zest of 1 orange
2 tablespoons fresh orange juice
1 tablespoon white wine vinegar
1 teaspoon kosher salt
¼ teaspoon cayenne pepper (or as much as you like)

Combine all of the ingredients in a small bowl and give them a good mix.

MARINATE THE BEETS

Pour ½ cup of the vinaigrette over the beets and toss well. (You'll use the rest to dress the endive.) Let the beets marinate for 30 minutes.

PUT IT ALL TOGETHER

2 small endives or 1 head radicchio, separated into leaves
Remaining vinaigrette
Pot-Roasted Beets
1 tablespoon chopped fresh oregano
1 tablespoon fresh mint leaves (tear any larger leaves)
⅓ cup pistachios, almonds, or hazelnuts (the same nuts used to make the oil), toasted (page 17)

Lay out the endive or radicchio on a platter, then drizzle with the remaining vinaigrette. Set the beets here and there on the endive and scatter the herbs and nuts over the top.

BEET CAPONATA

A few years back, while I was cooking at an event at a Sonoma winery, I was elbow deep in a menu that cried out for caponata but it was early spring, months before eggplant would be in season. My friend Emma Lipp brought me a box of vegetables that had been pulled from the winery's garden. Among them were some good-looking beets, nice red onions, and celery. I had the inspiration that the beets could take the place of eggplant in a caponata with celery and red onions. The big takeaway here is to use the same oil to serially fry all the ingredients, building flavor in the oil each time you reuse it. Serve with grilled bread.

SERVES 4

MAKE THE POT-ROASTED BEETS

Cook the beets, peel, and break them up with your fingers as directed on page 148; put them and any liquid the beets have given up in a medium bowl.

MAKE THE CAPONATA

1 cup olive oil
⅓ cup slivered almonds
Pot-Roasted Beets
4 garlic cloves, cut into ⅛-inch-thick slices
3 celery stalks, halved lengthwise and cut into 1-inch lengths
Pinch or two of kosher salt
1 medium red onion, roughly chopped
8 anchovy fillets, roughly chopped
2 tablespoons capers
½ teaspoon crushed red pepper flakes

Combine the oil and almonds in a small saucepan and heat over medium heat, stirring, so that the nuts toast evenly. When they smell toasty—about 3 minutes—drain the almonds in a sieve set over a bowl and add them to the beets. Pour the almond-infused oil through a paper towel–lined strainer (to remove the leftover nut bits, which could burn the next time you use the oil) into another bowl, then return the oil to the saucepan. Add the garlic and cook over medium heat until faintly golden; keep the garlic chips moving so they don't burn. They don't have to be crunchy, just browned. Drain as above, add the garlic to the bowl of beets, and toss.

Return the oil to the saucepan, add the celery, and season with a pinch or two of salt. Sauté the celery over medium heat for about 5 minutes, until the celery is softened but still retains a little crunch in the middle. Remove the celery with a slotted spoon (you want to leave the oil behind for the onion) and add to the beets.

Add the onion to the pan, season with a pinch or two of salt, and sauté over medium heat until softened but not limp, 3 to 5 minutes. Remove the onions with a slotted spoon and add to the beets.

Reduce the heat under the pan to low. Add the anchovies, capers, and red pepper flakes and cook, swirling them in the oil, until the anchovies have disintegrated. You can help them along by smooshing with a wooden spoon. Pour the anchovies and all the oil into the bowl with the beets and mix everything together.

PUT IT ALL TOGETHER

1 ½ tablespoons sugar, or to taste
1 tablespoon red wine vinegar
¼ cup fresh basil leaves, chopped
Caponata
Kosher salt

Add the sugar, vinegar, and basil to the caponata and mix with a big spoon. Adjust the salt if needed.

BEETS *with* TOASTED SEEDS, PICKLED JALAPEÑO, *and* CILANTRO

One night, I found myself lost in a reverie of all the superb food I had eaten on a trip to Oaxaca City. It occurred to me that I hadn't seen any beets during my trip (a little meander around the internet confirms that there are beets aplenty in Oaxaca, so it just must have been bad luck), but I wondered how they might have been prepared in a true Zapotec kitchen in that ancient city. This is my Oaxaca-inspired creation, with lots of crunchy toasty seeds, pickled spicy peppers, fresh citrus, and picked herbs.

SERVES 4

MAKE THE POT-ROASTED BEETS

Cook the beets, peel, and break them up as directed on page 148; put the beets and any liquid the beets have given up in a medium bowl.

PUT IT ALL TOGETHER

1 tablespoon chopped jarred or canned pickled jalapeños
1 teaspoon kosher salt, or to taste
A few drizzles of olive oil
Grated zest and juice of 1 to 2 limes (to taste)
Pot-Roasted Beets
2 cups fresh cilantro leaves
Toasted Mixed Seeds (page 18)

Add the jalapeños, salt, olive oil, lime zest, and juice to the beets and toss well. Scatter some of the cilantro and seeds all over a serving plate, then arrange the beets on top. Scatter the rest of the cilantro and seeds over the beets. Finish with a random drizzle or two of olive oil.

BEETS *with* WATERCRESS *and* HORSERADISH SAUCE

Beets and horseradish are a time-honored marriage in which the sweet and tender beets are counterbalanced by the breathtaking punch of horseradish. The sauce is as simple as could be.

SERVES 4

MAKE THE POT-ROASTED BEETS

Cook the beets, peel, and break up as directed on page 148; put them in a bowl with any liquid the beets have given up.

MAKE THE HORSERADISH SAUCE

¼ cup sour cream

2 tablespoons prepared horseradish

1 teaspoon red wine vinegar

Kosher salt

Cracked black pepper—somewhere between 10 and 20 twists of a pepper mill, to taste

Combine all the ingredients in a bowl and stir to mix.

PUT IT ALL TOGETHER

A handful of watercress

1 tablespoon olive oil

1 teaspoon red wine vinegar

Horseradish Sauce

Pot-Roasted Beets

A chunk of peeled fresh horseradish for grating

Dress the watercress with the olive oil and vinegar. Smear the horseradish sauce over a platter. Lay the beets on the platter and scatter the watercress over. Grate some fresh horseradish on top.

whatever he was, it was organically grown.

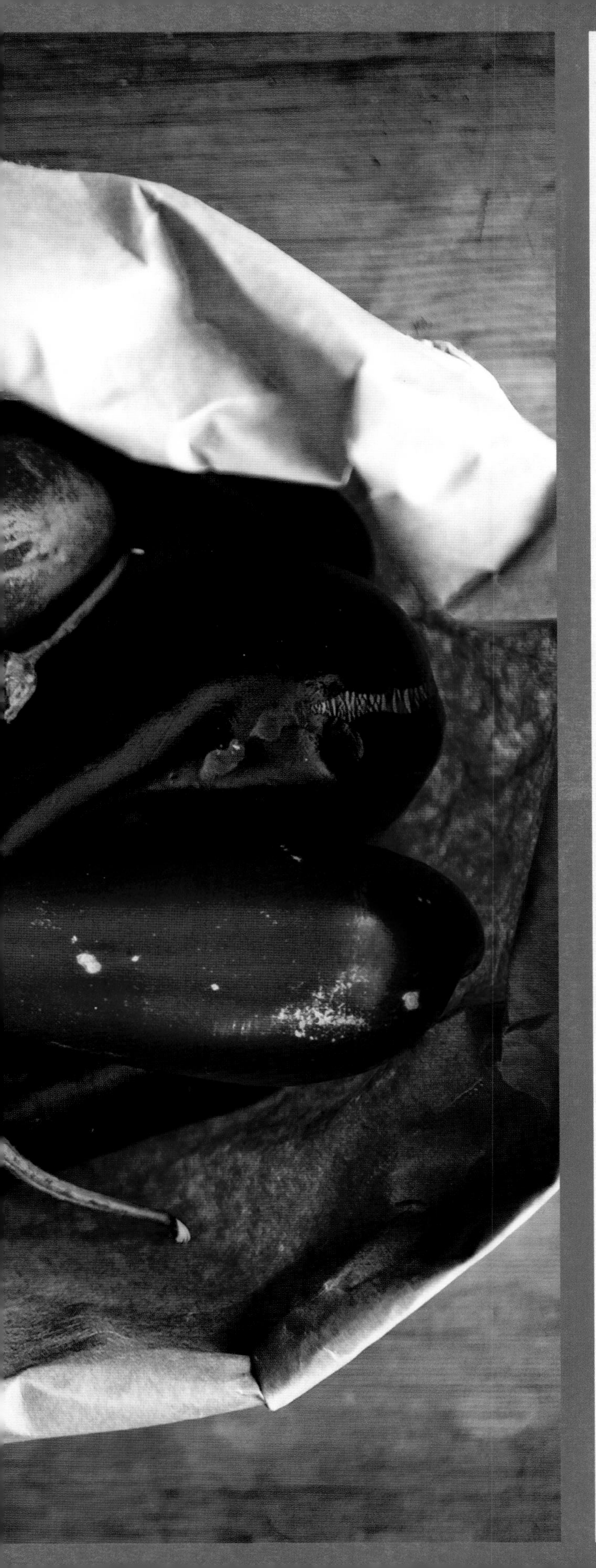

Fire-Roasted Eggplant

FIRE-ROASTED EGGPLANT

BASIC RECIPE

Cooking eggplant is as unpredictable as cooking an octopus or, for that matter, raising a child: They're all different and all require attention. Whether you cook eggplant over a stove, burner on a gas or wood grill, or even directly on the white coals of a campfire, the charred skin will lend a smoky effect.

Whatever method you choose, the eggplant must be handled gently so that its skin doesn't break. Using tongs is fine, but don't test for doneness by sticking it with a knife or pricking it with a fork because the meat of the eggplant steams inside its own skin, cooking more evenly and more gently than it would if the flesh were exposed to direct heat. Cooking times will vary, but you will know the eggplant is done when the skin is wrinkly and the flesh yields to the touch; it should feel soft all over. If you are not sure, cook it a bit longer (it's hard to overcook eggplant).

Note: *A 2-pound globe eggplant takes 10 to 15 minutes. Italian eggplants, which usually weigh about half a pound, take around 10 minutes. Very slim Japanese eggplants take about 5 minutes.*

SERVES 4

1 globe eggplant (about 2 pounds) or 4 small Italian eggplants (about ½ pound each)

Place the eggplant(s) on a grill over high heat or cook directly on a gas burner turned to medium high. Turn the eggplant from time to time to char on all sides. When the eggplant is done, the skin will typically have turned darker purple, almost black, and it will puff up and then collapse a bit. Give it a squeeze to be sure it's tender. Set aside in a bowl to cool. Gently peel the eggplant. If there are a few little flecks of black or burned skin left here and there, that's fine.

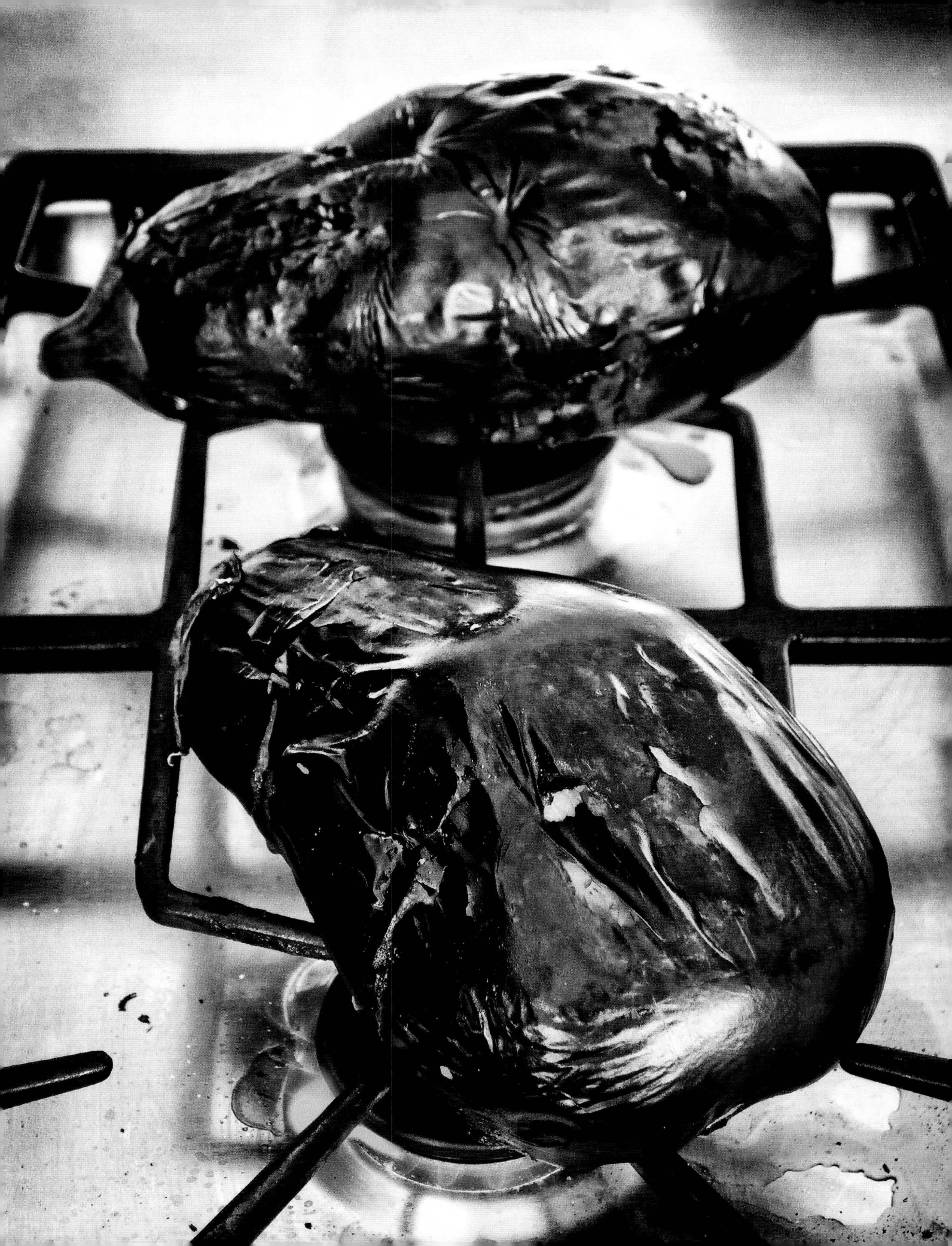

ROASTED EGGPLANT *with* HERB DRESSING

You can serve this in lots of different ways, but you can't go wrong with grilled bread. Pita or crackers are fine too. You could also make a plate of grilled summer vegetables and this mashed roasted eggplant. It's a good match for roasted leg of lamb or goat, and it's pretty nice on a plate with a fish fillet—or on a picnic with roast chicken.

Note: *Sichuan peppercorns enhance flavor by creating a sensation between numbing and tingling on your tongue. They are available in Asian markets, online, and in many supermarkets. I prefer the stronger effect of the less-common green ones, but the reddish ones are fine here too.*

SERVES 4

MAKE THE FIRE-ROASTED EGGPLANT (PAGE 158)

MAKE THE HERB DRESSING

1 teaspoon Sichuan peppercorns, preferably green
½ cup fresh flat-leaf parsley leaves, minced
½ cup fresh mint leaves, minced
2 to 3 garlic cloves, grated or minced and mashed to a puree with some salt (page 70)
2 teaspoons kosher salt, or to taste
2 tablespoons oil from Oil-Poached Garlic or Shallots (page 20) or olive oil
Grated zest and juice of 1 lemon

Buzz the Sichuan peppercorns in a spice grinder or pulverize them using a mortar and pestle. Mix the pepper, herbs, garlic, salt, oil, zest, and juice in a bowl.

PUT IT ALL TOGETHER

Fire-Roasted Eggplant
½ cup olive oil, or as needed
Herb Dressing
2 teaspoons kosher salt, or to taste
Pita, crackers, or bread for serving

Put the eggplant in a bowl and add the olive oil and herb dressing. It will look as if there's a lot of oil in the bowl, but eggplant is a sponge and it will absorb the oil and become all the more delicious for having done so. Holding a fork in each hand, pull the eggplant apart into strands, tossing to form a magnificent mound. If the mixture readily absorbs all the oil, drizzle a bit more in. Season with the salt. Let the eggplant sit at room temperature for an hour or two. It will keep in the fridge for at least a day.

Serve with pita, crackers, or breads.

EGGPLANT *with* TAHINI *and* BASIL

A few years back when I was in Tel Aviv, a visit to the home of an affable woman named Irit (I never did get her last name) provided one with the simplest and best lesson in eggplant roasting. As she cooked, she shared the narrative of her life and stories about her past, as well as insights into Israeli cooking. All the while, she was cooking a big eggplant over the gas flame of her stove. Eventually she removed the eggplant from the flame, peeled it, and set it on a plate on top of a puddle of tahini loosened into a delicious sauce with water and lemon juice. The dish was memorable in both its simplicity and its exquisite taste and texture.

SERVES 4

MAKE THE FIRE-ROASTED EGGPLANT

4 Japanese eggplants

Roast the eggplants as described on page 158.

PEEL AND DRESS THE EGGPLANT

Fire-Roasted Eggplant
A few drizzles of olive oil
Kosher salt

Peel the cooked eggplant, using their stems as handles. You can clip the stems off if you like, but I usually leave them on for this recipe because they will hold their shape better. Lay the eggplants side by side on a platter, drizzle some olive oil over, and sprinkle with salt to taste. (At this point, you can put the eggplant in the fridge for a day or two, where it will continue absorbing oil and salt, growing more delicious. Warm in a 300°F oven before serving; cooked eggplant is very forgiving about rewarming.)

MAKE THE TAHINI SAUCE

3 tablespoons tahini, plus more if needed
1 large garlic clove, peeled and minced or grated
2 tablespoons fresh lemon juice
2 tablespoons water, plus more if needed
1 tablespoon olive oil
1/4 teaspoon salt

Although there are just a few ingredients in this sauce, getting the proportions right can be a little tricky because the consistency of store-bought tahini varies. Combine the ingredients in a mixing bowl and whisk together. Add a little more water if the sauce is too thick, or a little more tahini if it's too loose; it should be a little looser than Heinz ketchup. The sauce is good in the refrigerator for a couple of days, but it will thicken as it sits and will need to be adjusted with water.

CONTINUED

MAKE THE BASIL SAUCE

½ cup fresh basil leaves, roughly chopped
2 tablespoons olive oil

Work the basil and oil using a mortar and pestle until you create a fine paste, adding the oil a little at a time to keep the paste moving like pesto. If you are mortar-and-pestleless, mince the basil with a knife and combine with the oil.

PUT IT ALL TOGETHER

Tahini Sauce
Fire-Roasted Eggplant
Kosher salt
Basil Sauce
A squeeze of lemon
8 lemon cheeks (below)

Smear the tahini sauce all over a platter. Lay the eggplant on the sauce. Sprinkle with some salt. Spoon the basil sauce over the eggplant, then finish with the lemon juice. Serve with the lemon cheeks.

LEMON CHEEKS

By using "lemon cheeks," rather than lemon wedges, you can avoid getting seed/pits in your lovingly prepared recipe. To make lemon cheeks, cut a lemon lengthwise into thirds, from stem to stern. The outer two parts are the cheeks, so called because they look like, to be completely honest, butt cheeks. Make sure to pluck out any seeds in the cheeks before serving them. The remaining third has lots of juice, so don't throw it out. Squeeze the juice through a strainer and save for whatever.

EGGPLANT *with* GREEN BEANS *and* TOASTED WALNUTS

Eggplant and walnuts are a common pairing in Middle Eastern and North African cuisines. This is an exceedingly simple dish, which is always a good thing to my way of thinking.

SERVES 4

Preheat the oven to 350°F.

MAKE THE FIRE-ROASTED EGGPLANT

1 small globe eggplant or 2 Italian eggplants (about 1 pound total)

Cook the eggplant as directed on page 158. Cool, peel, and mash with a fork. You will need 1 cup mashed eggplant for this recipe.

MEANWHILE, BLANCH THE BEANS

1 pound green or yellow beans, or a combination of the two, stems trimmed
1 ½ teaspoons kosher salt, or to taste

Bring a large pot of water to a rolling boil. Add the beans and cook just until soft to the tooth—taste them as you go and make a judgment call, this will probably take 4 to 7 minutes. Drain the beans in a colander and spread out to dry on a kitchen towel. Sprinkle with the salt.

TOAST THE WALNUTS

½ cup walnuts

Roughly chop the walnuts and spread on a small baking sheet. Toast in the oven for about 5 minutes; they're done when they've darkened a little and the kitchen smells like toasted nuts. Set aside.

DRESS THE EGGPLANT

1 cup mashed Fire-Roasted Eggplant
¼ cup fresh basil leaves, chopped
2 Oil-Poached Garlic cloves (page 20), minced
2 tablespoons oil from Oil-Poached Garlic (page 20) or olive oil
¼ teaspoon kosher salt, or to taste
Juice of 1 lemon

Put the eggplant in a large bowl, add the basil, garlic, garlic oil, salt, and lemon juice, and mix well with your hands or a fork.

PUT IT ALL TOGETHER

Dressed Fire-Roasted Eggplant
Blanched green beans
Toasted walnuts
Kosher salt
Fresh lemon juice

Add the beans to the bowl and mix them with the eggplant. Have at it; you want the eggplant mixture to really coat the beans. (Once again, I prefer hands for this, they're just more effective for thoroughly integrating the ingredients.) Add the walnuts and mix again. Season with salt and lemon juice. Eat a bean or two to check for salt and acidity, and make whatever adjustments your mouth recommends.

SWORDFISH *with* SWEET, SOUR, *and* SPICY EGGPLANT

Some pairings are just meant to be and, to me, eggplant and swordfish are one of them. This is a versatile dish, as delicious eaten cold out of the fridge as it is hot off the stove. The swordfish is cut into cubes, cooked just right, and nestled into the eggplant. This is another recipe where, like the Beet Caponata (page 150), I fry ingredients serially in the same oil, building more flavor each time I add a new one. It's delicious the day you make it and no less so the next—ideal picnic food.

SERVES 4

MAKE THE FIRE-ROASTED EGGPLANT (PAGE 158)

COOK THE CELERY

4 celery stalks
2 tablespoons oil from Oil-Poached Garlic or Shallots (page 20) or olive oil
Kosher salt

Trim the celery and slice lengthwise in half. Cut into squarish pieces about ¾ inch long.

Heat the oil in a large skillet over medium-high heat. When you see a wisp of smoke, add the celery, season with a pinch of salt, and toss or stir as if you're making a stir-fry until the celery turns a lovely light green, about 2 minutes. You want celery that is softened but still a little crunchy. Remove the celery to a plate to cool.

COOK THE VEGETABLES

1 cup olive oil
3 garlic cloves, thinly sliced
2 tablespoons capers, drained and dried on a paper towel
1 medium onion, thinly sliced
Kosher salt
1 medium fennel bulb, trimmed and thinly sliced
3 tablespoons tomato paste
1 teaspoon crushed red pepper flakes
10 anchovy fillets, chopped
¼ cup red wine vinegar
2 tablespoons sugar
5 to 10 fresh basil leaves, roughly chopped

Set a strainer over a small heatproof bowl. Combine the olive oil and sliced garlic in a medium saucepan set over medium heat. As the garlic colors, swirl it around in the oil so it cooks evenly; when it's golden brown, pour the oil and garlic into the strainer. Transfer the garlic to a small plate and return the oil to the pan. Add the capers and cook for 3 to 4 minutes, then pour the oil and capers into the strainer. Transfer the capers to the plate and return the oil to the saucepan. Add the onion, season lightly with salt, and cook for 5 to 8 minutes, until softened but still with some bite. Pour into the strainer, then set the onions aside and return the oil to the saucepan. Add the fennel, season lightly with salt, and cook for 8 to 12 minutes, until mostly but not entirely soft. Add the tomato paste and red pepper and cook, stirring, until the tomato paste darkens slightly, 2 to 3 minutes. Add the anchovies and cook, stirring, until they have broken down. Add the red wine vinegar, sugar, and the garlic, capers, onion, celery, and basil and cook, stirring, for 3 minutes to blend all the ingredients. Remove to a bowl to cool.

MAKE THE SWORDFISH

1 ½ pounds swordfish steaks, about 1 ½ inches thick
2 tablespoons canola or grapeseed oil
1 teaspoon kosher salt

Preheat the oven to 400°F.

Remove any skin from the swordfish and trim away the bloodline (dark part). Cut the swordfish into roughly 1 ½-inch chunks. Heat the oil in a wide ovenproof skillet over medium-high heat. When you see a wisp of smoke, put the swordfish chunks in the pan and brown on the first side; shoot for a light brown color on that side, 2 to 3 minutes.

Once you see good color, put the pan in the oven to finish cooking the fish, 6 to 8 minutes. The cubes of fish should feel firm but with a little give in the center. Use a metal skewer such as a cake tester or a meat thermometer to pierce a cube at its thickest point; the skewer should feel quite warm when you touch it to your lip. Remove the fish from the pan and cool.

PUT IT ALL TOGETHER

Fire-Roasted Eggplant
Vegetables
Kosher salt
Swordfish
8 to 12 fresh basil leaves, roughly chopped

Put the eggplant in a bowl, add the vegetable mixture, and mix well, making sure all the oil is incorporated into the eggplant. Check for seasoning and add salt if necessary. Very gently toss the swordfish in the eggplant and vegetable mixture so the swordfish is nicely coated. Transfer to a platter and garnish with the basil.

SPLIT ROASTED EGGPLANT *with* SPICED GROUND LAMB

This is a good make-ahead dish for a party. I stuff eggplant with lamb, yogurt, raisins, and mint and spices. You can prepare everything in advance and then, about 15 minutes before you want to serve it, assemble the dish, bang it into the oven, and away you go.

SERVES 4

MAKE THE FIRE-ROASTED EGGPLANT (PAGE 158)

WHILE THE EGGPLANT COOLS, COOK THE LAMB

2 teaspoons sweet paprika
1 teaspoon kosher salt
½ teaspoon ground cumin
½ teaspoon ground coriander
½ teaspoon crushed red pepper flakes
12 ounces ground lamb
1 tablespoon canola oil
3 tablespoons raisins
1 heaping tablespoon chopped Oil-Poached Shallots (page 20)

Combine the paprika, salt, cumin, coriander, and red pepper flakes in a medium bowl, then add the lamb and mix well.

Heat the oil in a large skillet over medium-high heat. When you see a wisp of smoke, add the lamb; it should sizzle. Once the lamb browns, stir it and add the raisins. When the lamb is cooked, just a few minutes, remove with a slotted spoon, transfer to a bowl, and mix in the shallots; set aside. Save the fat in the pan for the dressing if you'd like.

MAKE THE YOGURT DRESSING

½ cup Greek-style yogurt or labneh
Juice of 1 lemon
2 tablespoons olive oil
2 tablespoons lamb fat from the skillet (optional)

Put the yogurt in a bowl and whisk in the lemon juice, olive oil, and lamb fat, if using. Whisk until smooth. Set aside.

SAUTÉ THE TOMATOES

2 tablespoons oil from Oil-Poached Shallots (page 20) or olive oil
6 to 8 ounces grape or cherry tomatoes
⅛ teaspoon crushed red pepper flakes
Pinch of kosher salt
About 3 tablespoons water

Heat the oil in a large skillet over medium-high heat. When you see a wisp of smoke, add the tomatoes, then add the red pepper and salt and give the pan a swirl. Cook until the tomatoes soften but don't totally collapse; some of the tomatoes will break down more than others. The process will take 3 to 5 minutes. Add enough water to the pan to deglaze it and make a sauce. Set aside.

MAKE THE MINT-ANCHOVY SAUCE

½ cup fresh mint leaves
4 anchovy fillets
¼ cup olive oil

Roughly chop the mint and anchovies together. Add the olive oil and mix.

PUT IT ALL TOGETHER

Fire-Roasted Eggplant
Kosher salt
Yogurt Dressing
Cooked lamb
Sautéed tomatoes
Mint-Anchovy Sauce

Preheat the oven to 350°F.

Cut open the eggplants, slicing them from stem to stern. Pinch each one open like a baked potato and set on a baking sheet. Season each one with a pinch of salt. Spread a spoonful of yogurt dressing on each eggplant, then spoon the lamb mixture on top, followed by the tomatoes.

Heat in the oven for 5 to 8 minutes, until the eggplant is warmed through. Spoon the mint sauce over, sprinkle with salt, and serve.

Covered-Pot Carrots

COVERED-POT CARROTS

BASIC RECIPE

My grandparents' garden had cherry tomatoes, sugar snap peas, lettuces, carrots, and so much more. I grew up a block away from them and hung out at their house a lot in the summer. My sister and I would yank carrots out of the ground by their tall leafy stems, give them a perfunctory rinse with the hose, and crunch away, using their stems as handles. To this day, I can't eat a raw unpeeled carrot without being transported back to that garden. Carrot skin is earthy and rich and adds greatly to the pleasure of carrot eating. A good scrub is all they need.

Here I cook unpeeled carrots in a lidded pot sealed with foil. This is the same technique that I use for beets, leeks, and spring onions, as well as pork shoulder. It's worth noting that the technique works just as well for large carrots as for smaller ones, and they'll be just as sweet, though they can take as long as 1½ hours. It's a cool reveal when, after a big fat carrot has cooked, you slice through the dull orange skin to reveal a brilliantly colorful interior.

SERVES 4

1 pound medium carrots
1 teaspoon kosher salt
1 teaspoon oil from Poached Garlic or Shallots (page 20) or olive oil

Preheat the oven to 300°F, with a rack in the middle.

Scrub the carrots to get the dirt off and cut off the stem ends. Toss the carrots with the salt and oil, then lay them out in a single layer in a Dutch oven or other heavy pot with a lid. Cover the pot with foil and seal by placing the lid on top of the foil.

Transfer the pot to the oven and cook the carrots, first checking after 30 minutes for doneness by poking one with a metal skewer; when the carrots are done, the skewer will slide in and out easily. If it doesn't, continue to cook, checking occasionally, until the carrots are done; each time you check them, move the carrots around a little and rotate the pot. When they are done, take the pot out of the oven and lay the carrots in a single layer on a plate to cool.

YOUNG CARROTS *with* SPRING ONIONS, SUMAC, *and* ANCHOVIES

As various vegetables make their march through the season, I have found they respond quite wonderfully to this preparation, especially when they are young and delicate and have just hit the market. Here carrots get a bracing wake-up from the combination of bright, lemony sumac, funky anchovies, and sweet spring onions. When spring onion season has passed, you can substitute scallions.

SERVES 4

MAKE THE COVERED-POT CARROTS AND SPRING ONIONS

1 pound young carrots
2 spring onions, split lengthwise in half (discard any dry or discolored tops)
1 teaspoon kosher salt
1 teaspoon olive oil

Cook the carrots and spring onions with the salt and olive oil as directed on the opposite page. Check the spring onions after 30 minutes; as soon as they are tender, remove them to a plate to cool. Cut the cooled carrots lengthwise in half.

MAKE THE HERB SAUCE

2 teaspoons oil from Oil-Poached Garlic (page 20) or olive oil
2 tablespoons chopped fresh parsley
2 tablespoons chopped fresh mint
1 garlic clove, grated or minced, or 2 Oil-Poached Garlic cloves (page 20), mashed
A few pinches of kosher salt

Mix all the ingredients in a small bowl.

PUT IT ALL TOGETHER

Covered-Pot Carrots and Spring Onions
Herb Sauce
Juice of ½ lemon, plus a squeeze
8 anchovy fillets
1 cup Crunchy Croutons (page 21)
2 teaspoons ground sumac

Toss the carrots and spring onions with the herb sauce and the juice of the ½ lemon. Lay the carrots and spring onions out on a serving plate. Drape the anchovies over them. Scatter the croutons over and shower with the sumac. Finish with a squeeze of lemon juice.

CARROTS *with* RICOTTA *and* PUMPKIN SEEDS

Sometimes a simple combination of just a few ingredients defines a recipe. This is one I make and eat happily all through the year. Ground fennel seeds plus honey pulls out the inherent sweetness in the carrots and the ricotta. The toasted pumpkin seeds add a crunchy, savory counterpoint.

MAKE THE COVERED-POT CARROTS (PAGE 172)

Cut the carrots lengthwise in half and then into pieces 3 to 4 inches long.

PUT IT ALL TOGETHER

1 1/2 cups ricotta
Heavy cream as needed
Kosher salt
Covered-Pot Carrots
Honey for drizzling
1/4 cup toasted pumpkin seeds (page 17)
1 1/2 teaspoons ground toasted fennel seeds (page 17)

Adjust the consistency of the ricotta as necessary (not all ricottas are equally thick) by whisking in a little cream until the ricotta is just slightly thicker than Hellmann's mayonnaise. Season with salt to taste.

Spoon nice globs of ricotta on a platter, then lay the carrots this way and that on top. Drizzle plenty of honey over everything. Using the flat of a chef's knife, crush—don't pulverize—the toasted pumpkin seeds. Sprinkle the seeds all over and finish with a dusting of the ground fennel seeds.

CARROTS *with* ORANGE *and* GOLDEN RAISIN SALAD

I've got more than a few memories of carrots, shredded or otherwise, served with orange juice concentrate and Sun-Maid raisins at potlucks in the 1970s and 1980s. None of these were particularly notable, so it was with some surprise that I found myself combining the same ingredients some thirty years later. This salad skews North African, with an array of spices and a handful of cilantro. It's also a green light to mix and match whatever citrus fruits you can get your hands on.

SERVES 4

MAKE THE COVERED-POT CARROTS (PAGE 172)

Cut the cooled carrots lengthwise in half.

PREPARE THE ORANGE AND RAISIN SALAD

⅓ cup sultana (golden) raisins
3 tablespoons white wine vinegar
2 oranges
3 to 4 tablespoons olive oil
1 to 2 teaspoons kosher salt (to taste)
½ teaspoon ground fenugreek
½ teaspoon ground cumin

Put the sultanas and vinegar in a small saucepan and heat over low heat for a few minutes so that the raisins bloom (soften and plump). Set aside.

Suprême (segment) the oranges: Using a sharp serrated or other knife, cut off the top and bottom of each orange to expose the flesh. Stand each one up on a cutting board and cut away the skin and bitter white pith in strips, working from top to bottom and following the natural curve of the fruit. Trim away any remaining pith. Then, holding the fruit over a bowl to collect the juice and using a sharp paring knife, cut down along the membranes on either side of each segment to release it, letting the sections drop into the bowl as you go. Squeeze the juice from the membranes into the bowl.

Add the sultanas and their liquid to the bowl and stir in the olive oil, salt, fenugreek, and cumin.

PUT IT ALL TOGETHER

Covered-Pot Carrots
Orange and Raisin Salad
1 teaspoon Aleppo pepper or a pinch of cayenne
½ cup fresh dill leaves, chopped
½ cup fresh cilantro leaves
½ cup slivered almonds, toasted (page 17)
Flaky sea salt

Toss the carrots together with the orange salad, pepper, dill, cilantro, and almonds on a serving plate. Finish with a sprinkling of flaky salt.

CARROTS *with* BACON, SAGE, *and* MAPLE SYRUP

In the shooting-fish-in-a-barrel department, if this isn't the perfect Thanksgiving side dish, then, as the old blues song says, "Grits ain't groceries, eggs ain't poultries, and Mona Lisa was a man." Fine for Christmas and Easter too.

SERVES 4

MAKE THE COVERED-POT CARROTS

1 pound medium carrots
1 teaspoon olive oil
12 fresh sage leaves, minced
1 piece star anise

Cook the carrots as directed on page 172, adding the sage leaves and star anise to the pot. Cool, then cut the carrots into bite-sized pieces. Put the carrots and sage in a large bowl.

MAKE THE BACON

6 ounces slab bacon or thick-cut bacon
1 to 2 teaspoons vegetable oil

Cut slab bacon into chunks the size of a large almond or slice thick-cut bacon into ½-inch-wide pieces.

Slick a large skillet with the oil, add the bacon, and set over medium heat. Cook the bacon until nicely browned but not too crunchy, stirring occasionally as you go; it'll take about 10 minutes. Transfer the bacon to the bowl of carrots; I like to add a tablespoon or two of the bacon fat as well.

PUT IT ALL TOGETHER

Covered-Pot Carrots
Cooked bacon
2 tablespoons maple syrup
1 to 2 tablespoons red wine vinegar
Kosher salt

Toss the carrots and bacon with the maple syrup and vinegar. Check for salt and serve.

CHARRED CARROTS *with* ALMONDS *and* CHERVIL *(or Another Herb)*

I would love you to try this with chervil if you can find it (or grow it). When I think of how cilantro was a rarity not too long ago, I believe there is hope for us chervil lovers. Chervil is a member of the carrot family and its feathery tendrils resemble carrot tops. Its taste—somewhere at the meeting place of anise and parsley—brightens the flavor of carrots. If you can't find chervil, feel free to substitute parsley and tarragon or parsley and dill.

SERVES 4

MAKE THE COVERED-POT CARROTS

2 large shallots, peeled
1 pound medium carrots
1 teaspoon kosher salt
1 teaspoon olive oil

Cook the carrots as directed on page 172, adding the shallots to the pot.

CHAR THE CARROTS

1 tablespoon vegetable oil
Covered-Pot Carrots

Heat the oil in a large skillet over high heat. Add the carrots and char, turning occasionally, for 1 to 2 minutes per side. Remove from the heat.

PUT IT ALL TOGETHER

Charred carrots
Cooked shallots (above)
½ cup fresh chervil leaves or a mix of fresh flat-leaf parsley and dill or tarragon leaves, chopped
⅓ cup almonds, toasted (page 172) and crushed with the flat of a chef's knife
Juice of 1 lime
1 tablespoon oil from Oil-Poached Garlic or Shallots (page 20) or olive oil
1 tablespoon chili oil
¼ teaspoon ground cumin
¼ teaspoon kosher salt

Combine all the ingredients in a bowl. Serve on a platter.

SOFT LEEKS

SOFT LEEKS

BASIC RECIPE

Cooking in a sealed heavy, lidded pot is a simple and foolproof method that I use time and again. This basic technique will make your kitchen life much easier. The beauty of the cooking method is that it yields leeks that are soft-to-the-tooth with great depth of flavor and no burnt edges (which often happens with roasted or sautéed leeks). They are smooth, sweet, and creamy. And I have yet to find a simple poached or grilled fish fillet or piece of chicken that doesn't waltz terrifically with them.

SERVES 4

4 medium leeks
2 tablespoons olive oil
½ to 1 teaspoon kosher salt (to taste)

Preheat the oven to 250°F.

Cut off the tough green tops and the roots of the leeks. Slice the leeks lengthwise in half and rinse thoroughly to get out all the dirt, fanning the layers like a pack of cards, but keeping each half intact. Shake off excess water over the sink.

Toss the leeks with the oil and salt, then lay them out in a single layer in a Dutch oven or other heavy pot with a lid. Cover the pot with foil and place the lid on top. Transfer to the oven and cook for 30 minutes. Check the leeks to see how they are progressing by poking them with a metal skewer. If they are super tender, they're done. If not, continue to check the leeks every 10 minutes or so until they are; this may take as long as 60 minutes in all.

Serve the leeks immediately, or transfer to a container, cover, and refrigerate. They will keep for several days. Rewarm before serving.

BRAISED LEEKS *with* BROWN BUTTER–LEMON SAUCE

I love hollandaise, and I've made a mind-boggling amount of it for restaurant brunches, but at home I skip all the emulsifying. The result is a simpler sauce but with all the contrasting and complementary flavors of a hollandaise, here folded into an herbaceous leek and bread salad.

SERVES 4

MAKE THE SOFT LEEKS (OPPOSITE)

MEANWHILE, MAKE THE CROUTONS

2 slices bread of your choice, torn into large (about 1 ½-inch) pieces

¼ cup olive oil

½ teaspoon kosher salt

Preheat the oven to 400°F.

Toss the torn bread with the olive oil and salt and spread out in a single layer on a baking sheet. Bake for about 10 minutes, until golden brown. Transfer to a plate.

MEANWHILE, COOK THE 6-MINUTE EGGS

5 large eggs

Boil the eggs for 6 minutes as directed on page 241. Peel.

MAKE THE BROWN BUTTER–LEMON SAUCE

Brown Butter made from 4 tablespoons unsalted butter (page 22)

Grated zest and juice of 1 lemon

¼ teaspoon kosher salt

3 dashes Tabasco

One 6-Minute Egg

Rewarm the brown butter, if necessary, then combine with the lemon zest and juice, salt, and Tabasco. Using a fork, smash the egg and then whisk into the brown butter mixture.

PUT IT ALL TOGETHER

Soft Leeks

Croutons

½ cup mixed fresh tarragon and flat-leaf parsley leaves, chopped

Splash of olive oil

Kosher salt

Remaining four 6-Minute Eggs

Brown Butter–Lemon Sauce

Rewarm the leeks. Combine the croutons, leeks, herbs, and olive oil in a bowl. Toss gently, ideally with your hands, and season with salt. Lay out on a platter. Tear the eggs in half or in quarters and scatter evenly around. Spoon the sauce over everything.

LEEKS *with* BUTTER *and* BLACK PEPPER

This recipe might as well be titled How I Got Black Pepper Back. My mother taught me that if you pass the salt, it's impolite to do so without passing the pepper. I took this automatic two-step routine—reaching for the pepper mill just after sprinkling salt—to heart well into my career as a professional cook. Eventually, I grew so used to the pepper that I no longer tasted it, so I basically stopped using it.

On a recent family trip to Mexico, we visited Puebla, a culinary wonder of a city, where I ordered something called *cebollas al vapor* ("steamed onions") with a meal. When it arrived at the table, it appeared to be nothing more than a steamy bowl of sliced yellow onions speckled with bits of black pepper. Those onions, which turned out to be cooked in water with just a hint of pork fat and garnished with nothing more than a generous amount of pepper (and a squeeze of lime) turned out to be the star in seven days of eating adventures.

When I got home I rummaged through the spice cabinet, pulled out my long-neglected pepper mill, and filled it with fresh peppercorns. I steamed some onions, gave them a heavy dusting of black pepper, and finished them with lime. The dish sang. Here I've substituted leeks for the yellow onions and butter for pork fat, but feel free to use whichever you prefer. Chicken schmaltz would do the trick as well.

MAKE THE SOFT LEEKS (PAGE 182), SUBSTITUTING 2 TABLESPOONS BUTTER OR CHICKEN OR PORK SCHMALTZ (FAT) FOR THE OIL

PUT IT ALL TOGETHER

Soft Leeks
A healthy pinch of ground black pepper
A squeeze or 2 of lime

Transfer the leeks to a platter, season with the pepper and lime juice, and serve.

GRILLED FENNEL SAUSAGE *with* SOFT LEEKS *and* BITTER GREENS

Cooked leeks, like onions, have a comforting sweetness. The fennel seeds in Italian sausage have an affinity for that sweetness. Starting the sausages on the stovetop lightly colors the casings, and finishing them in the oven makes them succulent—much juicier than frying them in a skillet. Mustard greens have the sharpness of prepared mustard, plus some peppery freshness; I think the ideal mustard green for this is the Scarlet Frill. If you can't find mustard greens, arugula, watercress, or blanched broccoli rabe will give you the texture and bracing flavor you're looking for.

SERVES 4

COOK THE SOFT LEEKS (PAGE 182)

MEANWHILE, MAKE THE MUSTARD VINAIGRETTE

2 teaspoons Dijon mustard
1 tablespoon white wine vinegar
Pinch of kosher salt
3 tablespoons olive oil

Whisk together the mustard, vinegar, and salt in a bowl. Slowly whisk in the olive oil.

COOK THE SAUSAGES

1 tablespoon canola or grapeseed oil
4 sweet Italian sausages with fennel seeds

Remove the bottom oven rack and preheat the oven to 400°F.

Heat the oil in a large skillet over medium heat until you see a wisp of smoke. Add the sausages (no need to move them at all while they brown). After 3 to 4 minutes, turn the sausages over and place the skillet on the oven floor. Cook for 6 to 8 minutes, until cooked through but still juicy. Remove the sausages to a plate and set aside.

PUT IT ALL TOGETHER

Soft Leeks
Mustard Vinaigrette
⅓ cup mixed fresh herbs (such as tarragon, mint, and flat-leaf parsley), roughly chopped
Sausages
A handful of mustard greens

Put the leeks in a large bowl, dress with most of the vinaigrette, and toss with some of the herbs. Taste for salt and season if necessary. Place the majority of the leeks on a serving plate. Slice the sausages in half on an angle and scatter on top of the leeks. Place the remainder of the leeks and more of the herbs on top of the sausages. Lightly dress the mustard greens with the remaining vinaigrette, scatter over the leeks and sausages, and shower with the remaining herbs.

LEEKS *with* LEMONY RICOTTA *and* HAZELNUTS

A bright lemony vinaigrette shines like a ray of summer sunlight in a wintry meal. A mix of herbs—any herbs—heightens the illusion.

SERVES 4

COOK THE SOFT LEEKS (PAGE 182)

MEANWHILE, PREP THE LEMONY RICOTTA

2/3 cup ricotta cheese
Grated zest of 1 lemon
1 tablespoon fresh lemon juice

Combine the ingredients in a bowl and set aside.

MAKE THE LEMON VINAIGRETTE

Grated zest and juice of 1 lemon
1/4 teaspoon kosher salt
1/4 cup olive oil

Combine the zest, juice, and salt in a bowl. Whisk in the olive oil and set aside.

PUT IT ALL TOGETHER

Lemon Vinaigrette
Lemony Ricotta
1/4 cup hazelnuts, toasted (page 17) and cracked with the flat of a chef's knife
Soft Leeks
1/3 cup mixed fresh herbs (such as tarragon, flat-leaf parsley, and mint), chopped

Drizzle half the lemon vinaigrette over the ricotta. Dress the leeks with some of the remaining vinaigrette. Smear some of the ricotta over a platter and place the leeks on top. Scatter the remaining ricotta, the herbs, and hazelnuts on top. Drizzle any remaining vinaigrette over the platter.

LEEK *and* MARROW GRATIN

Rich, savory, and luxurious, bone marrow is humble yet elegant. You can simply roast the bones, scoop out the marrow, and eat it on toast with some crunchy salt. I do it that way myself sometimes, but I also like mixing the marrow with soft leeks, aromatic spices, and fresh herbs—flavors that are a counterpoint to the buttery, beefy taste of the marrow. The crunch of bread crumbs adds a pleasing textural element to each bite.

Note: *Some markets sell marrow bones already split lengthwise in half. If yours does not, ask the butcher to do it.*

SERVES 4

COOK THE SOFT LEEKS (PAGE 182)

ROAST THE BONE MARROW

2 (6-inch-long) marrow bones (see note), split lengthwise

¼ teaspoon kosher salt

Preheat the oven to 350°F.

Put the marrow bones cut side up on a baking sheet and sprinkle with the salt. Roast for about 20 minutes, until the marrow softens and can be scooped from the bones. Scoop it into a bowl and let it cool. Reserve the bones.

MAKE THE MARROW FILLING AND STUFF THE BONES

Soft Leeks, cooled

Bone marrow (from above)

1 teaspoon chopped fresh thyme, savory, or rosemary

Pinch of ground mace or nutmeg

Pinch of ground black pepper

Slice the leeks against the grain into ⅛-inch-wide slices. Chop the bone marrow and transfer to a bowl. Add the leeks, then stir in the remaining ingredients. At this point, you can refrigerate the leeks and marrow for 2 to 3 days; refrigerate the bones too.

When you are ready to finish the dish, spoon the leek mixture into the channels of the marrow bones. (If there's any filling left over, it's nice spread on toasts as a crostino or added to risotto.)

MAKE THE BREAD CRUMBS

⅓ cup panko bread crumbs (because these are exactly the right size)

⅓ cup oil (your choice), or if you're feeling it, 5 tablespoons unsalted butter

Pinch of kosher salt

Set a small strainer over a bowl. Combine the panko and oil (if using butter, melt it first and then add the crumbs) in a small skillet set over medium heat. Cook attentively for a few minutes, stirring, until the panko is golden, then drain in the strainer. Toss with the salt and set aside.

PUT IT ALL TOGETHER

Stuffed marrow bones

A handful of watercress or other sharp greens

Juice of ½ lemon

1 tablespoon olive oil, or to taste

¼ teaspoon kosher salt

Bread crumbs

4 lemon cheeks (page 163)

Preheat the oven to 450°F.

Put the stuffed bones on a baking sheet and roast for 7 to 10 minutes, until the filling is very hot.

While the bones are in the oven, combine the greens, lemon juice, oil, and salt in a bowl and toss.

Serve the bones, showered with the panko crumbs, on a platter along with the dressed greens and lemon.

GRILLED ASPARAGUS

GRILLED ASPARAGUS

BASIC RECIPE

You've probably been told to trim asparagus where the stalk wants to break apart. Nice-sounding idea, but it doesn't hold up in the real world. A much better rule of thumb is to cut the end off about 1½ inches above the point where pale starts to turn a darker green. As for the age-old thin versus thick debate, I resolutely choose both—and often at the same time.

Note: *If you don't have an outdoor grill, a hot cast-iron grill pan on your stove will do the trick.*

SERVES 4

2 to 3 pounds asparagus, trimmed and well rinsed
Olive oil
Kosher salt
Squeeze of lemon

Fire up the grill (I like charcoal, but gas works fine); you want medium-high heat.

Put the asparagus in a bowl and, using your hands, coat it with just enough oil so that the stalks are slippery. Shower lightly with salt. Place on the grill: Put the thicker pieces over the hotter spots and, as you might guess, the thinner pieces over the less hot spots. After 3 to 4 minutes, roll them over. Your aim is to cook the asparagus spears all the way through while developing a decent amount of char. You can check doneness by flexibility—the sweet spot is well short of limp. (Tasting works too.) Serve with a squeeze of lemon.

GRILLED ASPARAGUS *with* ROBUST HERB SAUCE

Asparagus always seems to show up at the time of year when you're feeling like a restless ten-year-old cooped up indoors on a sunny day. It is the surest bellwether of the season, the first vegetable that can give you a chewable mouthful. It also marks the first time most of us want to grill outside, so I celebrate my chance to char something . . . *anything.* All of the asparagus recipes in this book feature an herb sauce because, providentially, when asparagus first shows up in the markets, it arrives alongside tender local herbs.

It doesn't matter to me if asparagus is served hot, warm, or at room temperature. You can grill it well in advance of serving it. And it is one spring green that isn't the least bit shy about accepting big flavors. This green sauce is proof par excellence. The fresh herbs include parsley and tarragon, which ally with the earthiness of asparagus.

SERVES 4

MAKE THE ROBUST HERB SAUCE

1 brimming cup fresh flat-leaf parsley leaves, minced

1 tablespoon minced fresh tarragon

1 to 2 pinches of Aleppo pepper or crushed red pepper flakes

2 anchovy fillets, minced and smashed with the flat of a knife

1 garlic clove, grated or minced and mashed to a puree with a little salt (page 70)

1 small shallot, minced

Grated zest of 1 lemon

¼ cup plus 2 tablespoons olive oil

Toss the herbs, pepper, anchovy, garlic, shallot, and zest together in a bowl. Add the olive oil and mix together. The herbs will absorb some of the olive oil, so the green sauce will thicken a bit if you let it stand.

MAKE THE GRILLED ASPARAGUS (PAGE 192)

PUT IT ALL TOGETHER

Grilled Asparagus, cooled

Robust Herb Sauce

Juice of 1 lemon

A few drizzles of olive oil

Put the asparagus on a platter and, using your hands, gently mix with the herb sauce and lemon juice. Drizzle a bit of olive oil all over.

And thus it all began.

GRILLED ASPARAGUS *with* GRATED EGG

Mimosa is a classic technique named after the way a grated garnish of sieved hard-cooked eggs resembles the blossom of the mimosa tree. I first saw it at Il Cantinori, a wonderful Italian restaurant in Manhattan's East Village. I saw a waiter grating an egg onto someone else's plate. I asked for the same, but he told me it was only for preferred customers. That grumpy waiter threw me to my own resources, so the next time I prepared asparagus, it was for this recipe, and I've been mimosa-izing ever since.

SERVES 4

COOK THE 9-MINUTE EGGS

4 large eggs

Boil the eggs for 9 minutes as directed on page 241. Peel.

MAKE THE GRILLED ASPARAGUS (PAGE 192)

MAKE THE ROBUST HERB SAUCE (PAGE 194)

PUT IT ALL TOGETHER

Grilled Asparagus
Robust Herb Sauce
Juice of 1 lemon
Kosher salt
9-Minute Eggs

Gently toss the asparagus with the herb sauce and lemon juice. Add salt if you think it needs it. Roughly grate the eggs over the asparagus.

GRILLED ASPARAGUS *with* SPRING ONIONS *and* RAMPS

A party for spring vegetables—no other season need apply. If you have some fiddlehead ferns and morels, invite them to the festivities.

SERVES 4

PREPARE THE RAMPS AND ONIONS

6 ramps, trimmed

4 spring onions or 2 medium leeks, cut lengthwise in half and well rinsed

2 tablespoons good-quality olive oil

1 to 2 teaspoons kosher salt

Preheat the oven to 250°F.

Toss the ramps and spring onions or leeks with the oil, then lay them out in a single layer in a Dutch oven or other heavy pot with a lid. Cover the pot with foil and place the lid on top of the foil.

Slide the pot into the oven. Check the vegetables after 60 minutes; they should be super tender. Make a guess about how much longer they need—if at all—and reset your timer if necessary. Not all ovens are the same, and neither are all ramps and onions. The long, slow cooking removes every iota of sharpness, rendering the ramps and spring onions or leeks silky and soft. When they are done, remove from the oven and set aside. (Or cover and refrigerate; they will keep for several days. Save the juices for a gravy or sauce.)

MEANWHILE, MAKE THE GRILLED ASPARAGUS (PAGE 192)

MAKE THE PARSLEY-MINT-TARRAGON SAUCE

½ cup fresh flat-leaf parsley leaves, chopped

½ cup fresh mint leaves, chopped

1 tablespoon chopped fresh tarragon

Grated zest of 1 lemon

2 to 3 tablespoons olive oil

Mix the herbs, zest, and olive oil in a small bowl.

PUT IT ALL TOGETHER

Grilled Asparagus

Parsley-Mint-Tarragon Sauce

Ramps and onions or leeks

Put the asparagus on a platter and toss with the herb sauce. Rewarm the ramps and spring onions or leeks, add to the asparagus, and toss again.

GRILLED ASPARAGUS *with* DILL-CILANTRO SAUCE *and* CRISPED HAZELNUTS *(or Almonds)*

We often think of dill as a Scandinavian herb, and cilantro as a companion to chilies in Mexican or Thai food. You will, however, find the combination of the two in many Middle Eastern recipes. It is one I have always loved.

SERVES 4

MAKE THE GRILLED ASPARAGUS (PAGE 192)

MAKE THE DILL-CILANTRO SAUCE

1 brimming cup fresh dill leaves, chopped
1 brimming cup fresh cilantro leaves, chopped
Grated zest of 1 lime
¼ cup plus 2 tablespoons olive oil

Put the herbs in a bowl and stir together with the lime zest and olive oil.

PUT IT ALL TOGETHER

Grilled Asparagus
Dill-Cilantro Sauce
Juice of 1 lime
1 cup hazelnuts or almonds, toasted (page 17) and roughly pulsed in a food processor

Put the asparagus on a platter and gently mix with the herb sauce and lime juice, then scatter the nuts all over.

GRILLED ASPARAGUS *with* DILL-PARSLEY SAUCE *and* VERY SOFT SCRAMBLED EGGS

Richard Olney was a great cookbook writer, a home cook par excellence, and one of my guiding stars. He left his native America for the South of France, where he lived for many years, and the recipes he produced there are a model of clarity. This is my take on his soft scrambled eggs, which he engagingly described as "the softest of barely perceptible curds held in a thickly liquid, smooth, creamy suspension." Although he scrambled his eggs in a *bain-marie* (double boiler), I think you'll agree this skillet method gets it done.

Note: *Eggs cooked using this method (for that matter, almost all beaten eggs cooked in a pan) are best eaten immediately, so be sure to have all the other components prepped and at the ready. As soon as the eggs are finished, serve.*

SERVES 4

MAKE THE GRILLED ASPARAGUS (PAGE 192)

MAKE THE DILL-PARSLEY SAUCE

1 cup fresh dill, leaves chopped
1 cup fresh flat-leaf parsley leaves, chopped
Grated zest of 1 lime
¼ cup plus 2 tablespoons olive oil

Combine all the ingredients in a medium bowl and set aside.

MAKE THE SCRAMBLED EGGS

4 large eggs
2 tablespoons heavy cream

Whisk the eggs and cream together. Set a small heavy-bottomed skillet (not nonstick) over very low heat, pour in the eggs, and whisk slowly. As the eggs thicken, curds will form, about 2 minutes. If the curds form too rapidly, take the pan off the heat and continue to whisk slowly, then return to the heat. The eggs should be the consistency of very loose cottage cheese.

PUT IT ALL TOGETHER

Grilled Asparagus
Dill-Parsley Sauce
Juice of 1 lime
Scrambled Eggs

Gently toss the asparagus with the herb sauce and lime juice. Put the asparagus on a platter and mound the eggs on top.

Roasted Mushrooms

ROASTED MUSHROOMS

BASIC RECIPE

Here's what you need to remember when cooking mushrooms: They respond well to the application of heat . . . or at least the right heat for the right amount of time. Raw mushrooms can feel dry and squeaky in the mouth. But once they have yielded to the heat, they become pliable and silky. They slide over your tongue as smoothly as an oyster on the half-shell. If you continue cooking them at a reasonably high heat, mushrooms will take on a corona of crispiness as they caramelize. A little of this crispiness can be good; a lot, not so much. My method is simple. I put them on a parchment-lined baking sheet, drizzle them with oil, and sprinkle salt over them, then pop them into the oven and leave them until they're done.

SERVES 4

PREPPING MUSHROOMS

Any of the following mushrooms will work in this recipe. Here's how to prep them.

- ***Chanterelles:*** Trim the stems.
- ***Enoki and beech mushrooms:*** Break into small bunches.
- ***Maitake (hen of the woods) mushrooms:*** Trim the knobbly root ends. You don't have to take off much, just the bits that seem overly dense. Roughly separate the mushroom mass into florets.
- ***Portobello mushroom caps:*** Slice into ½-inch-thick slabs.
- ***White button or cremini mushrooms:*** Cut into quarters.

1 pound mushrooms, prepped as described above

2 to 3 tablespoons canola or grapeseed oil

Kosher salt

Preheat the oven to 425°F, with a rack in the upper third. Line a baking sheet with parchment paper.

Put the mushrooms on the parchment-lined baking sheet and gently toss with the oil. Lightly salt them and spread out on the baking sheet.

Slide the baking sheet into the oven to roast. Check after 7 minutes but, depending on the mushroom, they will often need more time; some will take up to 15 minutes. When they are done, they should be slithery and juicy with some caramelization and a meaty chew. Remove from the oven.

MUSHROOM SANDWICHES *with* ROSEMARY AIOLI

No meat here, but the hearty box gets checked with mushrooms, crunchy bitter greens, and an aioli whose creamy smoothness supports the pungency and heat of garlic and cayenne and the brininess of olives. Then add rosemary, an herb that can be counted on never to get lost in the background.

SERVES 4

MAKE THE ROASTED MUSHROOMS (OPPOSITE)

MAKE THE ROSEMARY AIOLI

1 large egg yolk
2 tablespoons water
2 garlic cloves, grated or minced
Pinch of kosher salt
Pinch of cayenne pepper, or to taste
1 cup Rosemary-Infused Oil (page 20)
15 Kalamata olives, pitted and chopped

Put the egg yolk, water, garlic, salt, and cayenne in a food processor and run for 30 seconds to 1 minute, until well blended. With the processor running, slowly drizzle in the rosemary oil in a *very thin stream* until the mixture begins to thicken, then add the rest of the oil in a steady slightly thicker stream. When the aioli has almost reached the consistency of store-bought mayo (not quite that thick, but it will stand up in peaks), add the chopped olives and pulse just long enough to mix in the olives. Scrape down the sides, transfer to a bowl, and set aside.

BLANCH THE GREENS

4 to 8 branches broccoli rabe or broccolini (1 or 2 per sandwich)
Kosher salt

Bring a large pot of water to a boil. Drop in the greens and cook until soft to the tooth, 3 minutes or so. Drain and lay the greens out on a kitchen towel; it's important that they are fairly dry or the sandwich will be soggy. Sprinkle with salt to taste.

PUT IT ALL TOGETHER

1 baguette or other long loaf
Roasted Mushrooms
Blanched greens
Rosemary Aioli
½ lemon

Preheat the oven to 400°F.

Warm the baguette in the oven for 5 minutes. Meanwhile, warm the mushrooms and greens together in a large skillet over medium heat.

Remove the bread from the oven, cut into sandwich lengths, and then split open. Spread the aioli on the cut sides like you mean it: Don't hold back. Stuff the sandwiches with the greens and mushrooms. Finish each with a squeeze of lemon and close the sandwiches.

ROASTED MUSHROOMS *with* WILTED GREENS

A combination of roasted mushrooms, blanched or quickly sautéed greens, and a variety of toasted seeds has become a go-to vegetarian dish at my restaurant. I love it with some hard cheese grated over the top. Here the green is escarole. It is just as delicious with broccoli rabe or any of the leafy brassicas (for example, mustard greens, broccoli, or Brussels sprouts). It'd even be great with pea shoots or Swiss chard.

SERVES 4

MAKE THE ROASTED MUSHROOMS (PAGE 204)

MEANWHILE, COOK THE ESCAROLE

3 to 4 tablespoons oil from Oil-Poached Garlic or Shallots (page 20) or canola oil
2 garlic cloves, smashed and peeled
2 heads escarole (or other green; see headnote), thoroughly washed
Kosher salt
2 tablespoons minced peeled ginger
Crushed red pepper flakes (or not)
Juice of 1 lemon

Heat a large pot over high heat until it's very hot, then add the oil and garlic. As soon as the garlic begins to brown, 30 seconds or less, add the escarole. Cook, stirring vigorously, until the escarole has wilted but still retains some of its crunch, just a few minutes. (If you find it easier to do the escarole in 2 batches, that's fine.) Add salt to taste, the ginger, and the optional red pepper flakes to taste. Cook for 2 minutes, until the escarole has wilted a bit but retains a little crunch. Add the lemon juice. Check the seasoning and remove from the heat.

PUT IT ALL TOGETHER

Roasted Mushrooms
Escarole
½ cup Toasted Mixed Seeds (page 18)
Olive oil
¼ to ½ cup grated Parmigiano-Reggiano, pecorino, or other hard cheese (skip the cheese to go vegan)

Lay the mushrooms and escarole on a platter. Scatter with the seeds and drizzle a little oil over everything. Sprinkle the cheese all over.

ROASTED MUSHROOMS *with* HERBS *and* CELERY ROOT

Celery root browns up like a roast potato, but it has a more delicate texture and a sweet vegetal flavor. Bay leaf works beautifully with it—a perfect marriage, like dill and smoked salmon, or lime and avocado, or cold gin with an olive.

SERVES 4

MAKE THE ROASTED MUSHROOMS (PAGE 204)

ROAST THE CELERY ROOT

1 large or 2 small celery roots (about 1 pound total)
3 tablespoons canola or grapeseed oil
Kosher salt

Preheat the oven to 400°F.

Peel the celery root with a chef's knife, cutting off all the knobby bits. Cut the celery root into haphazardly shaped pieces about the size of small plums. Try to keep the pieces roughly the same size so that they all cook in about the same amount of time.

Heat the oil in a large ovenproof skillet over medium-high heat. Add the celery root, season with salt, and cook, tossing from time to time, until golden on at least one side, 3 to 5 minutes.

Put the pan in the oven and roast for about 15 minutes, until the pieces are soft all the way through. Take the skillet out of the oven (remember, the handle is hot!) and, using a slotted spoon, transfer the celery root to a plate. Carefully pour off the oil.

PUT IT ALL TOGETHER

2 tablespoons unsalted butter
4 sprigs of fresh thyme
2 bay leaves
Roasted celery root
Roasted Mushrooms
1/3 cup mixed fresh soft herbs (tarragon and chervil, cilantro or parsley, or dill), chopped
2 tablespoons fresh lemon juice

Set the skillet over medium-high heat and add the butter, thyme, and bay leaves. When the butter foams, add the celery root and mushrooms and baste a few times with the foaming herbed butter, until the butter has browned. Add the chopped herbs and lemon juice, toss, and serve.

BAKED EGGS *with* MUSHROOMS *and* MORNAY SAUCE

Many cultures have a baked egg dish: shakshuka in Israel, huevos rancheros in Mexico, shirred eggs in England, ouefs en cocotte in France. In this recipe, the combination of eggs, mushrooms, cheese, and cream make for an ur–comfort food that satisfies the same cravings as a good mac and cheese. The eggs are baked with a Mornay sauce (basically just cream, a little flour, and an Alpine cheese), roasted mushrooms, some spices, and a little splash of Madeira or sherry. Good for breakfast, lunch, or dinner. In other words, anytime.

SERVES 4

MAKE THE ROASTED MUSHROOMS (PAGE 204)

MEANWHILE, PREPARE THE SPICE MIX

½ teaspoon ground fennel
½ teaspoon ground coriander
½ teaspoon ground fenugreek
¼ teaspoon ground nutmeg
¼ teaspoon ground black pepper

Mix the spices in a small bowl.

MAKE THE MORNAY SAUCE

1 to 2 tablespoons unsalted butter
Spice Mix
1 tablespoon all-purpose flour
1 cup whole milk
1 ½ tablespoons dry Madeira or sherry
1 cup roughly grated Alpine cheese, such as Comté, raclette, or Gruyère, or, better yet, a similar local cheese

Foam the butter in a medium saucepan over medium heat. Add the spice mix and whisk for 30 seconds. When the spices bloom (become fragrant as their oils are released), add the flour, whisking, then continue to whisk for 2 to 3 minutes. Slowly add the milk, whisking constantly, and reduce the heat to low. Cook at a simmer, stirring frequently, for 5 to 6 minutes, until thickened. Whisk in the Madeira or sherry. Gradually add the cheese, whisking until it melts. Check for seasoning and remove from the heat.

PUT IT ALL TOGETHER

Roasted Mushrooms

Mornay Sauce

Up to ¼ cup milk if needed

4 to 8 large eggs (you be the judge, based on who's at the table)

Chopped fresh herbs (your choice; optional)

Preheat the oven to 400°F.

Heat a medium (9 inches or so) baking dish or ovenproof skillet in the oven and lay the mushrooms in it. If you have let the sauce stand for a while, reheat it and be aware that you may need to add some more milk to thin it. (It's important that both the sauce and baking dish be hot.) Pour the sauce over the mushrooms. Crack the eggs into a bowl and then pour the eggs into the baking dish. Neatness doesn't matter.

Pop the baking dish into the oven and set a timer for 10 minutes. When the timer goes off, remove and check for doneness; the final timing is up to you, based on how cooked you like your eggs. A chopped herb garnish wouldn't go amiss, but isn't mandatory. Serve hot.

LEAFY SALADS

LEAFY SALAD

BASIC RECIPE

This chapter is more about an idea than it is about a particular ingredient with variations. It's about salad dressing, about tasting as you work through a recipe, about handling delicate lettuces. Please note, it's important to choose a roomy bowl in which to toss your salad; a salad-making bowl is a work space, not a storage container. You've got to have space to move the lettuces around or they'll bruise, be unevenly dressed, or end up on the floor.

Toss your salad with your hands, as if you're handling something precious and fragile. Be gentle and thorough. Taste from the very beginning right through to the end of the salad-making process. Taste the lettuce, then taste the vinegar or lemon juice, the oil, the herbs, the salt as you go. Keep in mind that lettuces can only hold so much dressing and, in general, the more tender the lettuce, the less dressing it can support. Finally, eat the salad as soon as you've finished tossing it. The acidity and salt will go to work on tender lettuces and they will wilt quickly.

SERVES 4

4 ounces tender non-bitter lettuce, such as Boston, Bibb, red leaf, or mâche
2 tablespoons olive oil
1 tablespoon vinegar or fresh lemon juice
¼ to ½ teaspoon kosher salt (to taste)

The only way to tell if your lettuce is clean is to rinse and taste it. Swish the lettuce around in a bowl of water, then eat a leaf or two. If they're sandy, lift the leaves from the water, drain and refill the rinsing bowl, and rinse again; repeat if necessary until the leaves are clean. Pat or spin dry.

Put the lettuce in a large bowl and drizzle the oil and vinegar all over the greens. Sprinkle on the salt and, using your hands and being as gentle as if you were lifting a sparrow's nest full of newborn chicks, lightly toss the salad. Taste again. Add a little more of any ingredient you like and toss once more.

ON VINAIGRETTES AND EMULSIONS, OR, YOUR BROKEN VINAIGRETTE ISN'T BROKEN

In its simplest form, a vinaigrette is a mixture of oil and an acid (which always contains water). If you add a thickening or emulsifying agent—for example an egg, some cheese, or mustard—the oil and acid have a good chance of combining into what is called an emulsion. An emulsified vinaigrette doesn't taste better or worse than an unemulsified (or "broken") one, but it is creamier.

Some people feel they have failed when their vinaigrette separates or breaks. I think that's ridiculous. Using a broken vinaigrette is a choice, not a mistake. My favorite Caesar salad dressing was engineered by my father-in-law, Jay. It's a broken vinaigrette, and it's delicious.

THE OLNEY

Years ago, when I first caught the cooking bug, I devoured cookbooks. None inspired me more than Richard Olney's *Ten Vineyard Lunches*. His salads are as much about emotion as they are about vegetables. His starting point was, "What is ready to be picked in my garden? If it's hyssop, then pile on the hyssop!" More than anything, though, I've always carried with me his devotion to using a veritable riot of herbs—plenty of them and all different kinds at once. Rather than mixing a lot of greens, I prefer to use one kind of lettuce per salad. Keep the greens simple and go crazy with the herbs.

SERVES 4

2 handfuls tender non-bitter lettuce, such as Boston, Bibb, red leaf, or mâche
4 cups mixed fresh soft herb leaves (parsley, chervil, mint, tarragon, cilantro, basil, dill)
1 tablespoon olive oil
1 teaspoon vinegar (white or red, your call)
¼ teaspoon kosher salt

Put the lettuce in a bowl and add the herbs. Add the olive oil, vinegar, and salt.

Gently toss.

Fig 327B: Everything we ever Wished for.

FRISÉE SALAD

Bits and pieces of the herbs, nuts, and fruit in this version of frisée salad nestle in the frisée like berries in a bramble. The recipe can and should be modified to your whims in as many ways as you can imagine.

SERVES 4

WASH THE LETTUCE

1 head frisée

Clip off and discard the brown ends at the tips and at the root end of the lettuce. Frisée holds some silt, so it may require a few washings. Separate into leaves and pat dry.

MAKE THE VINAIGRETTE

1 ½ teaspoons ground coriander
½ teaspoon ground cumin
¼ cup Oil-Poached Shallots (page 20), chopped, plus ¼ cup of their oil or olive oil
¼ cup white wine vinegar
1 teaspoon kosher salt

Mix all the ingredients together in a small bowl. The vinaigrette can be made right before serving, but it will be even better if it rests for 24 hours. Cover and refrigerate; bring to room temperature before using.

PUT IT ALL TOGETHER

½ cup Greek-style yogurt or labneh
Juice of ½ lemon
Washed frisée
1 cup chopped dried apricots, dried cherries, or dates
1 brimming cup chopped fresh herbs (chives are nice too)
½ cup hazelnuts or almonds, toasted (page 17) and crushed
Vinaigrette
Squeeze of lemon (optional)

Mix the yogurt and lemon juice in a small bowl. Using the back of a spoon, spread it all over a serving plate. Put the frisée, dried fruit, herbs, and nuts in a large bowl and drizzle the vinaigrette over. Mix gently but thoroughly. Finish with a squeeze of lemon if needed. Pile on the plate.

ARUGULA, PEA, *and* RADISH SALAD

Along about Memorial Day and on into the first days of summer, arugula and peas of every description show up in the farmers' market. The blossoms of garlic and chives also make their short-lived appearance. Maybe some asparagus. And a radish or two. I feel truly vegetable-rich. In this season, when I'm out fishing for flounder, fluke, porgy, or blackfish, I'll glide Hazel Ann, my fishing boat, into the shallows that are often rippling with rafts of local edible seaweed, such as ogo and ulva. If you are near a coast, while you may not have the same sea vegetables, you will have some. Ask around until you find a local forager and learn which ones are suitable. If you don't have access to any seaweeds, press on; this is a worthy salad with or without them.

SERVES 4

WASH THE ARUGULA

4 ounces arugula (the big stiff, peppery stuff, not the baby stuff)

Put the arugula in a salad spinner and soak briefly in cold water, then drain. Soak again if necessary to remove any remaining grit, then drain and spin-dry.

COOK THE PEAS

2 cups green peas (frozen are fine), sugar snaps, and/or snow peas (whatever is available)
Kosher salt

If using snow peas and/or sugar snaps, pull off the tough fibrous strings.

Bring a large pot of water to a rapid boil. Blanch the green peas, if using, for 30 seconds, just enough to set the color. Remove them with a strainer and run under cold water to cool them. Drain and dry on a kitchen towel. Do the same with the snow peas and sugar snaps, if using. Your goal is bright, fresh, still crunchy vegetables. Toss with a hearty pinch of kosher salt.

PUT IT ALL TOGETHER

A handful of fresh ogo or other crunchy edible seaweed (see headnote; optional)
8 asparagus spears, preferably fat ones (optional)
Cooked peas
Washed arugula
1 tablespoon plus 1 teaspoon olive oil
2 teaspoons mild white wine vinegar, or to taste
Pinch of kosher salt, or to taste
2 radishes
4 chive flowers (in season)

Rinse the seaweed, if you have it, until you've gotten rid of all the sand.

If using asparagus, cut off the woody ends. Carefully slice the asparagus lengthwise on a mandoline into thin slices, thin enough to be flexible but not floppy, or use a vegetable peeler.

Combine the peas, arugula, asparagus, if using, olive oil, vinegar, and salt in a large bowl and gently toss. Be careful not to overdress the salad. The arugula is a barometer; it should remain stiff and fresh, not limp and soggy. Taste and adjust the salt and acidity if necessary.

Lay the salad on a serving plate. Scatter the seaweed over, if you have it, and grate the radishes over the top with a Microplane. Finish by sprinkling the chive flowers, if you have them, all around.

PLATE SALAD

Grandma Hazel had a salad in her recipe book that she called a plate salad. I don't know if that was her name or if it was from the "summer fun" issue of *Better Homes & Gardens* in 1954 or so, but everyone in the Baldwin household called it that. Over time, it came to mean anything that was a salad served on a big plate. I'm quite fond of this incarnation with green goddess dressing, fresh herbs, a generous shower of mixed seeds, and halved lightly pickled eggs to finish. Think of the herbs as another green—a full-fledged member of the salad—rather than an accent. Use tons of them.

COOK THE 7½-MINUTE EGGS

4 large eggs

Boil the eggs for 7½ minutes as directed on page 241. Peel.

MAKE THE PICKLING LIQUID AND PICKLE THE EGGS

1 cup white wine vinegar
3 cups water
1 teaspoon black peppercorns
1 bay leaf
3 tablespoons kosher salt
7½-Minute Eggs

Combine the vinegar, water, peppercorns, bay leaf, and salt in a large saucepan and bring to a boil, then turn off the heat and let steep for at least 20 minutes. Cool and transfer to a nonreactive container.

Drop the peeled eggs into the pickling liquid. Cover and refrigerate for at least 24 hours before serving. The eggs will keep for a few days in the fridge.

MAKE THE GREEN GODDESS DRESSING (PAGE 107)

PUT IT ALL TOGETHER

8 small heads Little Gem lettuce or 4 romaine hearts, washed and patted dry
6 medium radishes, thinly sliced
1 large cucumber or a few small Middle Eastern ones, cut into bite-sized pieces (not peeled)
Green Goddess Dressing
2 cups loosely packed fresh herb leaves (use the same mix as for in the dressing)
¾ cup pumpkin, sesame, or sunflower seeds, or whatever you have in your larder, toasted (page 17)
Avocado slices (optional)

Toss the lettuce, radishes, and cucumbers with the dressing in a large bowl. Add half of the herb mix and taste for salt and acidity; adjust as necessary. Put the salad on a serving plate. Cut the eggs in half and add to the plate. Finish with a scattering of the toasted seeds and the rest of the herb mix. Finish with avocado slices, if using.

WINTER CITRUS SALAD

Bright as floral bouquets, citrus cheers up the monotones of winter; think satsumas, blood oranges, pink grapefruits, Cara Cara oranges, Meyer lemons, tangelos. I make a salad with as many different kinds as I can lay my hands on. The sweet, yielding flesh of citrus fruits pairs well with chicories, the crunchy bitter family of greens that includes escarole, radicchio, and endive. This salad is a sculptural opportunity when the leaves are left a little bigger: Play with it, and you'll see what I mean.

SERVES 4

WASH THE GREENS

1 to 2 endives, ½ head radicchio, or 1 small head escarole

Trim the bottoms of the greens and separate the leaves. Wash and pat dry.

PREPARE THE FRUIT

4 cups segmented citrus, juices reserved

Cut the fruit into any shape and size you like. Reserve 2 tablespoons of the juice for the vinaigrette (drink the rest).

MAKE THE VINAIGRETTE

2 tablespoons reserved citrus juice
1 tablespoon fresh lemon juice
¼ teaspoon crushed red pepper flakes, or more to taste
¼ cup olive oil

Combine the citrus juice, lemon juice, and red pepper flakes in a small bowl. Whisk in the olive oil.

PUT IT ALL TOGETHER

Washed greens
Citrus fruit
⅓ cup pistachios, toasted (page 17) and lightly crushed
15 to 20 oil-cured olives, pitted and halved
Vinaigrette
1 teaspoon dried mint
4 ounces feta, sliced (don't worry if it crumbles a bit)
A few fresh sprigs of mixed herbs
¼ teaspoon kosher salt

Gently toss the greens, fruit, pistachios, and olives with the vinaigrette in a large bowl. Add the dried mint, feta, fresh herbs, and salt and toss again.

CHICKEN SOUP

CHICKEN BROTH

BASIC RECIPE

My family loves chicken soup nearly as much as I love making it. A truly great soup starts with a hearty broth. I always start with raw chicken, and I make sure to break as many of the bones as possible to let out all the rich flavors locked inside them. Chicken skin has flavor and collagen that gives body to the liquid. While I stick by a few commandments for the recipe (more on that below), I'm always tinkering with the flavors. I often use ginger, but seldom garlic. Chicken soup is a great place for leftover fennel stalks, and a splash of Pernod ramps up fennel's anise flavor. If I'm using onions, leaving the skin on adds color to the broth. And if I have a can of tomatoes open or half a ripe one in my fridge, it's nice to include that for a little acidity, color, and whatever other *je ne sais quoi* the tomato contributes. A little pork can go a long way in enhancing the richness of the broth—some bacon rind, a trotter, or some other odd pork part you have in the back of the freezer.

NED'S COMMANDMENTS

COOKING TIME: 2½ hours from the boil

CHICKEN WEIGHT: 3 to 3½ pounds

WATER: 1 gallon / 3 tablespoons kosher salt

MAKES 4 QUARTS

3 to 3½ pounds raw skin-on, bone-in chicken—a whole chicken cut up is great, or use chicken parts, backs, and wings

1 medium parsnip (and/or 1 celery root or carrot)

1 fennel bulb with stalks and/or 1 celery stalk

2 medium onions (and/or leeks)

Herbs, spices, and/or other add-ins of your choice (see Take Your Pick, below)

3 tablespoons kosher salt

4 quarts water

Break the bones of the chicken in several places. Slice all the vegetables about ½ inch thick. Put all the ingredients in a large pot. (Don't bother putting any herbs and spices in a sachet.) Bring the liquid up to a boil, then adjust the flame to maintain a gentle simmer and cook for 2½ hours.

Strain the broth; discard the solids. Some liquid will have evaporated during cooking, so add water to make 4 quarts—that's the proper amount to balance the salt. Cool, then store in the fridge for up to a week, or freeze for up to a month. When you remove it from the fridge, scoop off the flavorful fat (schmaltz) and store it separately to use as you would lard, butter, or oil.

TAKE YOUR PICK

There is a world of flavorful ingredients I have used at one time or another in my chicken broth (choose just a few): ginger (skin on); dried thyme, fenugreek, coriander, cumin, and/or black peppercorns; pigs' foot; ancho or guajillo pepper, or any of the smaller dried peppers; a serrano or jalapeño; spring onions; fresh thyme, tarragon, parsley, or cilantro stems; oregano or marjoram; fresh turmeric; chicken feet; a hunk of bacon or a prosciutto end; tomatoes or a tomato product; tomatillos.

Ruth Bader Ginsburg
Herstory in the making!

CHICKEN SOUP *with* EGGS

I'm obsessed with *tamagoyaki*, the Japanese omelet composed of many thin layers of egg. Making it takes some practice, maybe years, but the sentiment is reflected in the version in this dish, which I think of as an easily accomplished union of tamago and a rustic French omelet.

SERVES 4

MAKE THE CHICKEN BROTH (PAGE 224)

COOK THE OMELETS

4 large eggs

1 teaspoon soy sauce

½ teaspoon sesame oil

Pinch of kosher salt

2 tablespoons oil from Oil-Poached Garlic or Shallots (page 20) or canola or grapeseed oil

Whisk the eggs with the soy sauce, sesame oil, and all in a bowl. Heat 1 tablespoon of the oil in a small (8-inch) sauté pan or skillet over high heat until it shimmers and you see a wisp of smoke. Pour half the eggs into the pan and wait for about 10 seconds, until a thin layer of egg has set on the bottom of the pan. Using a spatula, pull the set eggs from the outside toward the center of the pan so they start to form ridges, then let the remaining wet egg run into the vacant space, like a river overflowing its banks. Repeat the process until eventually all the eggs are set and gathered up in a ridgy mass. Finish by flipping the omelet a few times in the pan, then turn out onto a plate. As soon as the omelet is cool enough to touch (eggs lose heat quickly), use your hands to roll it up into a tight cylinder, being careful not to break up the omelet. Leave it to firm up and cool, and repeat with the remaining eggs and remaining 1 tablespoon oil.

PUT IT ALL TOGETHER

Omelets

2 cups Chicken Broth

2 scallions, both ends trimmed, leaving just the light green part in the middle, and very thinly sliced

3 tablespoons small fresh cilantro leaves (if you have large leaves, tear into pieces)

1 tablespoon plus 1 teaspoons Toasted Mixed Seeds (page 18)

Slice the omelets into ¾-inch-wide pieces, 6 to 8 per omelet. Put 3 or 4 slices in each of four bowls. Heat the chicken broth and pour ½ cup into each bowl. Add the scallions, cilantro, and sesame seeds.

PEANUT *and* HONEY SOUP *with* CHICKEN THIGHS

Some years ago, I worked in a kitchen in Red Hook, Brooklyn, with a cook from West Africa. As cooks do, we traded stories about our favorite dishes from home. He told me about his mom's peanut soup. As a lover of peanuts in all forms—boiled, salted, smoked, or peanut butter spread on bread with honey—I was fascinated. After reading recipes for a bunch of different peanut soups from Africa and elsewhere, I came up with this.

SERVES 4

MAKE THE CHICKEN BROTH (PAGE 224)

MAKE THE PEANUT BROTH BASE

4 cups Chicken Broth
1 cup unsalted roasted peanuts
6 Oil-Poached Garlic cloves (page 20)
½ teaspoon crushed red pepper flakes
½ teaspoon ground cumin
1 teaspoon ground coriander

Put all the ingredients in a blender and blend until smooth.

MAKE THE SOUP

¼ cup canola or grapeseed oil
4 skinless, boneless chicken thighs, cut into bite-sized pieces
½ teaspoon kosher salt
½ medium onion, chopped
2 tablespoons tomato paste
Peanut Broth Base
Grated zest and juice of 1 lime

Set a large saucepan over medium-high heat and add the oil. Season the chicken thighs with the salt. When you see a wisp of smoke rising from the pan, add the chicken and cook, stirring from time to time, until it's golden on a couple of sides (don't go crazy—light gold is fine, and the chicken doesn't have to be cooked all the way through at this point). Remove the chicken and lower the heat to medium.

Add the onion to the pan and cook until very soft but not heavily browned. Lower the heat, tilt the pan, and spoon out about half of the fat. Add the tomato paste and cook, stirring frequently, for 2 minutes, or until it darkens slightly. Put the chicken back in the pan, add the peanut broth base, lime zest, and juice, and bring to a hard boil over high heat Then reduce to a simmer and simmer until the chicken is cooked through, about 5 minutes.

At this point, the soup can be cooled and refrigerated for several days; or, you can freeze it and serve it whenever. Thaw in the refrigerator and reheat gently.

PUT IT ALL TOGETHER

Soup
1 cup mixed fresh flat-leaf parsley and dill leaves, minced
¼ cup crushed peanuts
A nice drizzle of honey
A squeeze of lime if needed

Ladle the soup into four bowls. Garnish with the herbs and peanuts. Lightly drizzle the honey all over. Maybe add a squeeze of lime.

It all starts with a delicious broth.

SPICY CHICKEN SOUP *with* GINGER *and* ZUCCHINI

Ginger, chili flakes, and a healthy dose of turmeric turn the basic chicken broth into a chorus of bright and bracing flavors. Some sautéed onions and zucchini give it body. A fine light summer supper.

SERVES 4

MAKE THE CHICKEN BROTH (PAGE 224)

MAKE THE SOUP

2 tablespoons oil from Oil-Poached Garlic or Shallots (page 20) or canola or grapeseed oil

1 medium-large yellow squash or zucchini, cut into ¼-inch-thick rounds

1 small onion, thinly sliced

¼ cup finely chopped peeled ginger

2 tablespoons minced fresh turmeric or 1 tablespoon ground

1 teaspoon ground fenugreek

1 teaspoon crushed red pepper flakes

4 cups Chicken Broth

Kosher salt

Heat the oil in a large saucepan over medium heat. Add the zucchini, onion, ginger, turmeric, fenugreek, and red pepper flakes and cook, stirring frequently, until the onion softens, about 5 minutes. Add the chicken broth and simmer for 5 to 7 minutes, until the vegetables are cooked but not mushy. Check for salt and spiciness and adjust if necessary.

PUT IT ALL TOGETHER

1 lemon, halved

Soup

A handful of fresh cilantro or other soft herb(s) leaves of your choice, coarsely chopped

Squeeze the lemon juice into the soup, give it a stir, and ladle into bowls. Garnish with the herbs.

CHICKEN FAVA SOUP

I first ate pureed fava beans on a trip to Tel Aviv, where they are known as *ful*. There the puree is served like hummus, garnished with olive oil and a squeeze of lemon juice and accompanied by a grilled flatbread of some kind. I love things that are familiar and unfamiliar at the same time, and the ful was exactly that: hummus with a slightly different flavor and texture. It's easy to make and nice to have around for a quick snack, good for dipping carrots or pita. Here, it serves another purpose, turning the rich chicken broth into a hearty thickened bean soup.

SERVES 4

MAKE THE CHICKEN BROTH (PAGE 224)

COOK THE FAVA BEANS

1 cup dried fava beans

3 garlic cloves

Fenugreek, fennel, or coriander seeds; ginger, fresh or ground; or whatever strikes your fancy

4 cups water

Soak the beans in 2 quarts water for 24 hours, during which time they will double in size. Drain the beans.

Wrap the garlic and any spices in a square of cheesecloth and tie up into a sachet with kitchen twine. Put the sachet, beans, and 4 cups water in a small pot, bring to a simmer, and cook until the beans are soft to the tooth (probably no more than 30 minutes, or less—beans vary). Drain in a sieve set over a bowl. Save the cooking liquid and set the beans aside.

MEANWHILE, COOK THE CHICKEN

1 pound skinless, boneless chicken thighs and/or breasts, cut into large chunks

1 1/4 teaspoons kosher salt

3 tablespoons canola or grapeseed oil

Season the chicken with the salt. Heat the oil in a large saucepan over high heat until you see the faintest wisp of smoke rising. Add the chicken, then reduce the heat to medium-high. You want to hear the chicken sizzling comfortably but not smell it burning; adjust the heat accordingly. Cook the chicken, stirring occasionally, until cooked through, 8 to 12 minutes. Remove from the pan and let cool. Don't clean the pan; you want the brown bits and the chicken fat for the next step.

When the chicken is cool, shred it with a fork or your hands.

COOK THE SPINACH

About 8 ounces spinach, well washed

Kosher salt

Set the pan in which you cooked the chicken over medium-high heat, add the spinach, and season it with salt. Cook, stirring frequently, until the spinach wilts and is soft, about 3 minutes. Remove the spinach to a plate. Don't wash the pan.

MAKE THE SOUP

2 to 3 tablespoons oil from Oil-Poached Garlic or Shallots (page 20) or olive oil

½ medium onion, thinly sliced

2 teaspoons dried mint

1 teaspoon ground cumin

¼ teaspoon crushed red pepper flakes

Kosher salt

Cooked favas

1 cup fava-bean cooking liquid

4 cups Chicken Broth

Grated zest and juice of 1 lemon, or more to taste

Return the saucepan to medium-high heat, add the oil, and the onion, mint, cumin, red pepper flakes, and a little salt. Cook until the onion is quite soft but has barely browned, about 5 minutes. Add the favas and mash them with a fork or a sturdy whisk (it's fine if you leave the mashed favas a little chunky), then add the fava liquid, chicken broth, and lemon zest and juice and bring to a boil. Check for seasoning.

PUT IT ALL TOGETHER

Cooked spinach

Soup

Oil from Oil-Poached Garlic or Shallots (page 20) or olive oil

Swirl the spinach into the soup to warm it. Ladle the soup into bowls and garnish with a drizzle of oil.

CHICKEN *and* WINTER VEGETABLE BOILED DINNER

Many cultures have a version of boiled dinner: pot-au-feu in France, bollito misto in Italy, cocido in Spain, pho in Vietnam, tafelspitz in Austria, and, yes, boiled dinner in New England. They are all basically alike in that the technique involved is nothing more than cooking simple ingredients in broth or water. The result is very pure, unadorned flavor. Condiments and sauces finish them off.

Here I give that treatment to chicken. The cooking is long and slow. Success relies on probing and tasting ingredients as they cook so you can decide when to remove them and set them aside until the final assembly. All in all, this recipe takes about an hour, give or take, and requires that you pay at least mild attention throughout. But part of the fun is to cook things as slowly as you can.

This version is all about winter vegetables, but there's no reason you couldn't make a spring/early summer boiled dinner with sugar snaps, fresh favas, spring onions, and young carrots.

Note: *I often lean toward dark-meat chicken parts, since they're more succulent and juicy, but it's worth mentioning that, in my experience, this is actually the absolute best way to cook chicken breasts.*

SERVES 4

MAKE THE CHICKEN BROTH (PAGE 224)

SALT THE CHICKEN

1 ½ teaspoons kosher salt
1 ½ pounds chicken parts (legs, thighs, and/or breasts, your choice)

Salt the chicken, put it on a large plate, and refrigerate at least 2 hours (or as long as overnight).

MEANWHILE, BLANCH THE CABBAGE

¼ green cabbage, core intact
¼ cup kosher salt

Slice the cabbage into 4 slim wedges, keeping the core intact (that way, the wedges will hold together when you cook them). Bring 8 cups water to a boil in a large saucepan and add the salt, then lower the heat to a simmer and add the cabbage. Cook for about 7 minutes. Remove to a plate. (You'll finish the cabbage by sautéing it later.)

COOK THE VEGETABLES AND CHICKEN

8 cups Chicken Broth, plus more if needed
Salted chicken
4 garlic cloves, halved
1 large leek, split lengthwise, well rinsed, and trimmed
1 or 2 medium carrots, scrubbed
1 or 2 medium parsnips, scrubbed
4 Yukon Gold (or other waxy) potatoes, cut into halves or quarters
½ apple (don't worry about peeling or coring)

Pour the broth into a medium pot and bring to a slow simmer. Add the chicken, garlic, vegetables, and apple. The ingredients should be generously covered; add more broth if necessary. Cook until the vegetables are tender and the chicken is cooked through, removing each item to a plate as it is done. Breasts will take 20 to 25 minutes; dark meat about 30 minutes. Some of the vegetables may be done before the chicken and some may take longer. Discard the apple; it's just there for flavor. Set the broth aside.

MAKE THE GREEN SAUCE

½ cup chopped fresh flat-leaf parsley
2 tablespoons chopped fresh tarragon
10 to 12 fresh chives
2 anchovy fillets
½ teaspoon capers
3 tablespoons oil from Oil-Poached Garlic or Shallots (page 20) or olive oil
1 Oil-Poached Garlic clove (page 20), minced, or ½ teaspoon grated or minced garlic

Mince the herbs, anchovies, and capers. Stir into the oil, along with the garlic.

FINISH THE CABBAGE

1 to 2 tablespoons reserved chicken fat or unsalted butter
Blanched cabbage

Heat the fat or butter in a large skillet over medium-high heat. Add the cabbage wedges and cook, turning occasionally, until tender but not mushy, 4 to 6 minutes. Remove from the heat.

PUT IT ALL TOGETHER

About 2½ cups broth from the chicken and vegetables
Cooked chicken, cabbage, and vegetables
Green Sauce
Dijon mustard for serving
Crusty bread for serving

Heat the broth in a large skillet and briefly warm the chicken, cabbage, and other vegetables in it.

Thickly slice chicken breasts; cut legs or thighs into 3 or 4 pieces each. Put on a platter. Cut the parsnips and carrots lengthwise into halves or quarters. Arrange on the platter. Moisten everything with some of the broth and drizzle with the green sauce. Ladle ½ cup of the broth per person into small bowls to enjoy by itself before, during, or after digging into the platter of cooked chicken and vegetables. Pass the mustard on the side. Serve with crusty bread

Dressed Eggs

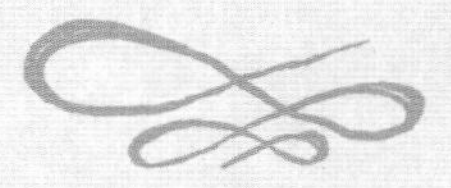

DRESSED EGGS

BASIC RECIPE

Why do I call them dressed eggs? Well, it all started at the restaurant one night, when I was headed down the stairs to make a mayonnaise, thinking we'd run a French classic called *oeufs mayonnaise* that night. Oeufs mayonnaise is simply boiled eggs garnished with mayonnaise and usually served with lettuce and/or herbs. I had the ingredients on hand for what I imagined would be a take on an herb mayo to accompany the boiled eggs: some capers, anchovies, and herbs. Midway down the stairs, I asked myself, "Why does this need to be a mayo? I can dress the eggs with those ingredients and leave out all the extra fat." That night we served the hard-boiled eggs with a piquant herbaceous dressing that is somewhere at the intersection of gremolata, chimichurri, and paradise. We liked it so much that in our kitchen shorthand it quickly became "egg candy," and thus it is called to this day.

You would not be misguided if you decided to double or triple the candy to have it on hand for grilled vegetables, grilled meats, or grilled anything. Truthfully, there are few things that can't be improved with a little egg candy. Ideally, make it a few hours before serving so that the olive oil picks up the mix of flavors.

SERVES 4

MAKE THE "EGG CANDY"

1 tablespoon oil from Poached Garlic or Shallots (page 20) or canola or grapeseed oil

1 teaspoon fresh marjoram or rosemary leaves

6 capers, minced

6 anchovy fillets, minced

2 Poached Garlic cloves (page 20)

Pinch of crushed red pepper flakes

1 tablespoon grated lemon zest

1 to 2 tablespoons olive oil, or just enough to loosen and moisten the mixture

Film a small skillet with the 1 tablespoon oil and heat over medium-high heat. Add the rosemary and marjoram and fry for about 30 seconds; as soon as the leaves start to color, remove from the pan.

Chop the herbs and put them in a small bowl. Add the capers, anchovies, garlic, red pepper flakes, and lemon zest and mix well, then add enough olive oil to give the mixture the consistency of a runny pesto. Taste for deliciousness. The flavors should be intense.

COOK THE 7½-MINUTE EGGS

4 large eggs

Boil the eggs for 7½ minutes as directed on page 241. Peel.

MAKE THE CROUTONS (OPTIONAL)

1 slice bread, about 1 inch thick

2 to 3 tablespoons olive oil

Kosher salt

Pull the bread apart with your fingers; the pieces should be just a little smaller than chocolate chips.

Set a large skillet over medium-high heat, add the oil and bread, and stir constantly until the croutons are mahogany in color; manage the temperature as necessary so the oil never smokes. Pour the croutons and oil into a strainer set over a bowl, then spread the croutons out on a paper towel. After a minute, toss the croutons with salt to taste.

CONTINUED

FRY THE PARSLEY (OPTIONAL)

1 tablespoon canola oil
¼ cup picked fresh flat-leaf parsley

You can use the same oil and pan in which you cooked the croutons. Heat the oil and check it with your laser thermometer if you have one; the ideal temperature for frying parsley is 320°F. Scatter the parsley in the pan and fry cook, about 30 seconds. Transfer the parsley to a paper towel.

PUT IT ALL TOGETHER

7½-Minute Eggs, cut lengthwise in half
Egg Candy
Croutons (optional)
Fried Parsley
Flaky sea salt

Arrange the eggs on a plate or small platter just big enough to hold them snugly. (Eggs are slippery and like to move around on the plate, so if they are packed in tight, they'll stay put until you serve them.) Dab about a half teaspoon of egg candy on each yolk. Scatter the croutons, if using, over them. Garnish with the parsley, sprinkle with flaky salt, and eat.

EGG-BOILING BIBLE

You might think that boiled eggs are too simple a recipe to put in a cookbook. But boiling an egg to a particular state takes some practice. Maybe you want a runny yolk, or maybe a yolk that's set; maybe a golden yolk, or one that's dry and pale, but without an unsightly gray halo. Each of these states of yolkness takes a specific amount of time but, contrary to popular belief, that amount isn't always the same. How many eggs are you cooking? How big is the pot and what's it made of? How big are your eggs? How powerful is the flame of your stove?

This guide—which evolved over the course of boiling twenty-eight billion eggs (it seems)—will help you master the art of egg boiling.

4 LARGE EGGS

In a saucepan, bring 2 quarts water (or enough to cover the eggs by 2 inches) to a rolling boil. Gently lower the eggs into the pan so they don't bang on the bottom. It will take a moment for the water to return to a boil. Once it does, lower the heat to a low boil/fast simmer and set your timer for 7½ minutes (for any of the recipes in this chapter), or for the desired time; see below. Meanwhile, prepare an ice bath. When the timer goes off, remove the eggs with a slotted spoon and transfer to the ice bath. Leave them there for 5 minutes, then tap them lightly to break the shells a bit so that water can seep in the cracks. I find that dipping the eggs in and out of cold water as I peel loosens the shells so that they come off more easily, but eggs have a mind of their own. Some are hard to peel, some aren't. Set the peeled eggs aside in a small bowl of water. Immersion helps eggs to keep their shape.

6 minutes (soft-boiled): The whites should be set, the yolks runny.

7½ minutes: The yolks should be barely set but moist and golden.

9 minutes (hard-boiled): A slightly controversial time for a hard-boiled egg, since most recipes call for 10 minutes. I like this timing because the yolk still has a hint of gold but is pretty much dry throughout.

7½-Minute Eggs

DRESSED EGGS *with* PEAS, CRÈME FRAÎCHE, *and* HORSERADISH

Horseradish's rapier thrust of sharpness wakes up the palate and complements broader flavors. In this recipe, peas, crunchy almonds, and velvety crème fraîche deliver their notes of garden freshness, crunch, and creaminess. As to whether or not to use fresh or prepared horseradish, that's a Solomonic choice. I don't choose between them and use a bit of each.

SERVES 4

COOK THE 7½-MINUTE EGGS

4 large eggs

Boil the eggs for 7½ minutes as directed on page 241. Peel.

COOK THE PEAS

4 or 5 sugar snap or snow peas

Blanch the peas in a small saucepan of boiling water until they turn a lovely shade of green, no more than 90 seconds. Cool them under cool running water or in a bowl of water with a few ice cubes. Drain and dry the peas, slice them on the bias about ¼ inch thick, and set aside.

MAKE THE ALMONDS IN BROWN BUTTER

2 tablespoons unsalted butter
1 tablespoon slivered almonds

Melt the butter in a small skillet. Add the almonds and proceed to make Brown Butter (page 22). Keep your eye on the almonds and, using a slotted spoon, remove them when they are a light khaki color. Keep the butter warm.

PUT IT ALL TOGETHER

2 to 3 tablespoons crème fraîche or sour cream
7½-Minute Eggs, cut lengthwise in half
Peas
Almonds in Brown Butter
Squeeze of lemon
Kosher salt
8 sprigs of fresh tarragon or chervil
Fresh and/or bottled horseradish

Smear the crème fraîche or sour cream over a small the plate and nestle the eggs in it, cut sides up. Scatter the peas and almonds over. Spoon the brown butter over the eggs and squeeze lemon juice over. Sprinkle a pinch of salt over each egg. Garnish with the herbs and finely grate a goodly shower of horseradish over everything, or spoon some bottled horseradish over, or do both.

DRESSED EGGS *with* PUMPKIN SEEDS, CHARRED PEPPER, *and* CILANTRO

Red bell peppers, roasted, peeled, chopped, and suspended in oil, are a great condiment for all sorts of things. Here they add a soft sweetness that contrasts nicely with toasty cumin and pumpkin seeds. You can adjust the spiciness of the dish to suit your taste. If you have toasted sunflower seeds or sesame seeds on hand, there's no harm in using them instead of pumpkin seeds. Better yet, throw a party for your seed collection and use them all.

SERVES 4

COOK THE 7½-MINUTE EGGS

4 large eggs

Boil the eggs for 7½ minutes as directed on page 241. Peel.

ROAST THE PEPPER

1 red bell pepper, poblano, or sweet Italian pepper
1 tablespoon oil from Oil-Poached Garlic or Shallots (page 20) or olive oil
A pinch or two of kosher salt

Roast the pepper on a grill or over a medium-high flame on your stove, turning occasionally, until it is charred all over and softened. Cool the pepper, then peel it. Discard the stem. Scrape out the seeds. Finely chop the pepper. Combine in a bowl with the oil. Season with salt and set aside.

PUT IT ALL TOGETHER

7½-Minute Eggs, cut lengthwise in half
Roasted pepper
A few sprigs of fresh cilantro
1 tablespoon pumpkin seeds, toasted (page 17)
¼ teaspoon cumin seeds
A few drizzles of oil from Poached Garlic or Shallots (page 20) or olive oil
Kosher salt
Red wine vinegar

Arrange the eggs cut sides up on a small plate, just big enough to hold them snugly. Spoon the roasted pepper on and around the eggs and strew the cilantro and pumpkin seeds over them. Sprinkle the cumin all over. Drizzle with the oil, season with salt, and finish with few drops of vinegar per egg.

DRESSED EGGS *with* CELERY *and* BOTTARGA *or* SALMON ROE

I like the poetic aptness of garnishing chicken eggs with fish eggs. Bottarga, if you haven't encountered it before, is pressed and dried fish roe (eggs), usually from mullet or bluefin tuna. I typically use mullet. You can find bottarga at the fish store or an Italian specialty store but, if you don't see it there, you can also get it online.

You'll likely have some bottarga left over after making this recipe. Don't worry, it keeps for a long time and tastes great grated over grilled vegetables, steak, or fish. Indeed, it's supernal with pasta. At times I have also replaced bottarga with salmon roe to great effect.

SERVES 4

COOK THE 7½-MINUTE EGGS

4 large eggs

Boil the eggs for 7½ minutes as directed on page 241. Peel.

COOK THE CELERY

1 celery stalk
Splash of olive, canola, or grapeseed oil

Cut off the white bottom end of the celery. Slice the stalk lengthwise in half, then slice on the bias into ¼-inch-wide pieces.

Heat a skillet over medium-high heat and add the oil. When you see the faintest wisp of smoke, drop in the celery and stir-fry for about 30 seconds. The goal is to get celery that's both soft and crunchy and a brilliant celadon green. Spoon the celery onto a plate lined with a paper towel.

PUT IT ALL TOGETHER

7½-Minute eggs, cut lengthwise in half
Cooked celery
Leaves from 4 sprigs of fresh flat-leaf parsley, chopped
Bottarga for grating or a few teaspoons of salmon roe (to taste)
1 lemon wedge
Flaky sea salt

Arrange the eggs cut sides up on a small plate, just big enough to hold them snugly. Scatter the celery and then the parsley over them. Generously shower with grated bottarga as you would with grated Parmesan—a healthy amount—or scatter the salmon roe over. (You can grate bottarga with anything from a Microplane to a potato peeler, depending on how subtle or strong you want it to taste. Myself, I like it either way.) Finish with a squeeze of lemon and some flaky salt.

DRESSED EGGS *with* PICKLED FISH

During fishing season in the Northeast, bluefish are often a sure bet, and they are a perfect pickling fish that pairs up well with the smooth, creamy texture of a dressed egg. You may not have access to fresh bluefish if you don't live in the Northeast. Or, just as likely, you might not want to go to the trouble of pickling your own. I get it. For those of you not as compulsively do-it-yourself as I am, store-bought pickled herring will do the trick. I promise you that the bracing flavor of the fish, along with a mayonnaise that is pepped up with anchovies, is a true taste explosion.

SERVES 4

COOK THE 7½-MINUTE EGGS

4 large eggs

Boil the eggs for 7½ minutes as directed on page 241. Peel.

MAKE THE ANCHOVY MAYO

3 anchovies
2 tablespoons mayonnaise
A chunk of pickled fish, about 1 inch square (see headnote and opposite)

Combine everything in a food processor and run until mostly smooth. Set aside.

PREP THE RADISHES AND CUCUMBERS

2 radishes
½ medium cucumber

Thinly slice the radishes on a mandoline or with a knife. Cut the cucumber into bite-sized pieces.

PUT IT ALL TOGETHER

Anchovy Mayo
7½-Minute Eggs, cut lengthwise in half
Radishes and cucumbers
4 ounces pickled fish (see headnote and opposite), cut into 8 bite-sized pieces
Squeeze of lemon
Poppy seeds, sesame seeds, and/or black sesame seeds for sprinkling
Flaky sea salt
Olive oil
A few sprigs of fresh dill

Smear the anchovy mayo over a small plate and lay the eggs on it, cut sides up. Combine the radishes, cucumbers, pickled fish, and lemon juice in a bowl, then scatter over and around the eggs. Finish with a sprinkling of seeds, a few pinches of flaky salt, and a drizzle of olive oil. Garnish with the dill.

PICKLED FISH

If you want to pickle your own fish, here's how I do it. This makes more than you will need for serving with dressed eggs. That's fine. It's nice for breakfast, lunch, or dinner, with some buttered rye bread.

CURE THE FISH

A 6-ounce bluefish or mackerel fillet, skin removed
½ teaspoon fennel seeds
½ teaspoon black peppercorns
A tiny piece of star anise
1 tablespoon kosher salt
1 tablespoon sugar
½ dried bay leaf, crumbled
Grated zest of ½ lemon

Remove the bloodline and any bloody flesh, as well as any pin bones, from the fish.

Toast the fennel seeds, peppercorns, and star anise in a small skillet over medium heat just until fragrant. Grind them in a spice grinder or with mortar and pestle, then combine with the salt, sugar, bay leaf, and lemon zest. Put the fish in a deep container and rub all over with the cure. Cover and refrigerate for about 12 hours.

MAKE THE PICKLING LIQUID

½ teaspoon fennel seeds
½ teaspoon black peppercorns
A tiny piece of star anise
⅓ cup Pernod, anisette, ouzo, or pastis (i.e., something in the licorice family)
3 cups water
2 cups white vinegar or white wine vinegar
1 bay leaf
3 tablespoons kosher salt
2 tablespoons sugar
Zest of ½ lemon removed in strips with a vegetable peeler

Toast the fennel, peppercorns, and star anise in a small saucepan over medium heat. When the fennel seeds have darkened slightly and the kitchen is redolent of spices, add the Pernod or other liqueur and turn off the heat. After 2 to 3 minutes, the residual heat will have cooked off the alcohol.

Add the water, vinegar, bay leaf, salt, sugar, and lemon zest to the pan and bring to a boil. Simmer for 5 minutes. Remove from the heat and let cool completely.

PICKLE THE FISH

Pour the cooled pickling liquid over the fish. Leave in the fridge for 24 to 48 hours. The fish can be refrigerated in its liquid for up to 1 week.

CHOCOLATE AND CREAM (GANACHE)

CHOCOLATE *and* CREAM (GANACHE)

BASIC RECIPE

Nothing satisfies a dessert craving more than dark chocolate. By knowing how to make a basic chocolate sauce of chocolate and heavy cream—*ganache* in classical cuisine—you'll be able to whip up all sorts of seductive desserts simply by adjusting the proportions of the two as appropriate.

The amount of cream relative to the amount of chocolate determines the consistency of a ganache. It's all about the proportions. So, in answer to a question my son, Irving, asked, "Yes, there is a use for ratios in real life."

Different recipes calls for different rations, but the method is always the same: Start by chopping the chocolate (70% to 80% cacao) into pieces the size of chocolate chips. Heat the cream to just below a simmer and let it stand for 5 minutes, during which time the temperature should drop to about 160°F. You can double-check with a thermometer to make sure you're in the ballpark. Pour the hot cream over the chocolate. Set a timer for 2 minutes, which will allow the chocolate to melt (it's important to be disciplined about this since the chocolate needs time to warm through so it will emulsify properly). Then slowly mix the chocolate with the cream. I use a whisk, but lots of people use a rubber spatula. Either works, but if you use a whisk, make sure to whisk gently, since the goal is just to integrate the chocolate and cream. Too much elbow grease will whip air into the ganache and change its texture.

You can use the ganache right away, but it can be stored in the fridge for about a week and in the freezer for a month.

After thousands of years, caffeine had no effect on him.

SLICED ICE CREAM SUNDAE *with* CHOCOLATE SAUCE, NUTS, SALT, *and* OLIVE OIL

I love when sweet and savory get all tangled up together. I often top ice cream with crushed nuts or croutons, flaky salt, olive oil, and even crushed red pepper flakes if the mood strikes.

I often find ice cream right out of the freezer hard to scoop. I sidestep the problem by slicing right through the cardboard pint container with a serrated knife, giving me ice cream disks. (This works only with cylindrical containers.) Then I just peel the cardboard off the ice cream. It's like a magic trick, very fast and clean (although you do have to take care not to cut yourself).

Once you have enough slices, place the lid of the ice cream container right onto the leftover ice cream in the container. The leftover ice cream will be better preserved this way than with the scooping method, which leaves air in the container.

SERVES 4

MAKE THE CHOCOLATE SAUCE

2 ounces dark chocolate (70% to 80% cacao)
½ cup heavy cream
Pinch of kosher salt

Chop the chocolate into small pieces and put in a bowl. Combine the cream and salt in a small saucepan and heat to just below a simmer. Remove from the heat and let stand for 5 minutes, or until the temperature drops to about 160°F.

Pour the cream over the chocolate and let stand for 2 minutes, then gently stir with a whisk or rubber spatula until it's combined and smooth.

SLICE THE ICE CREAM

1 pint ice cream (in a cylindrical container)

Take the lid off the pint and turn the pint on its side on a cutting board. Slice right through the top of the cardboard container, making a ¾-inch-thick disk of ice cream; then cut 3 more disks. Cover the remaining ice cream (there will just be a little left) and return to the freezer. Cut through the cardboard around each disk and peel it off. Set the slices of ice cream in chilled bowls.

PUT IT ALL TOGETHER

Sliced ice cream
Chocolate Sauce
⅓ cup nuts, toasted (page 17) and crushed
Olive oil for drizzling
1 teaspoon flaky sea salt

Garnish the ice cream slices with the chocolate sauce, nuts, olive oil, and salt.

HAZEL'S HOT CHOCOLATE

When we visited Venice last year, I arrived a day after my family. My daughter Hazel met me at the *vaporetto* (the ferry service that serves in lieu of surface transportation in Venice). At her urging, we stopped at a little bakery near our rental apartment. Characteristically, she already had the lay of the land and had made friends with the owner. She asked for a hot chocolate, "*Cioccolata, per favore*." Cool kid! It was generous and indulgent, completely unlike the skim milk and cocoa powder drink that is common here in the States. Hazel's drink was ganache in a coffee cup—nothing more, and nothing less.

SERVES 4

MAKE THE CHOCOLATE SAUCE (AKA HOT CHOCOLATE)

7 ounces dark chocolate (70% to 80% cacao)
1 ½ cups whole milk
½ cup heavy cream
2 teaspoons sugar
⅛ teaspoon ground cinnamon
Pinch of kosher salt

Chop the chocolate into small pieces and put in a bowl. Combine the milk, cream, sugar, cinnamon, and salt in a saucepan and heat to just below a simmer. Remove from the heat and let stand for 5 minutes, or until the temperature drops to about 160°F.

Pour the cream mixture over the chocolate and let it stand for 2 minutes, then gently mix together with a whisk or rubber spatula until combined and smooth. Pour into cups and serve.

SPICY GANACHE DIPPING SAUCE

There's no good reason why, after dinner, you can't gather around a bowl of warm chocolate sauce the way you gather around hummus or guacamole. Feel free to dip whatever you like (pretzels, strawberries, shortbread cookies, potato chips); I like it with baguette toasts. You can make a bigger batch of this and freeze some of it so that all you have to do when you're in a dipping-sauce kind of mood is warm it in a double boiler or microwave (heat it in brief bursts in the microwave, stirring after each one).

Note: *The sauce will keep for a week in the fridge or a month in the freezer.*

SERVES 4

MAKE THE TOASTS

1 baguette (you probably won't use the whole thing)
Olive oil or melted unsalted butter for brushing
Kosher salt

Preheat the oven to 350°F.

Cut the baguette into 16 to 20 (½-inch-thick) slices and brush them with the olive oil or melted butter. Salt lightly and toast on a baking sheet in the oven for 10 to 12 minutes, until crisp. Remove from the oven.

MAKE THE CHOCOLATE SAUCE

2 ounces dark chocolate (70% to 80% cacao)
½ cup heavy cream
½ teaspoon sugar
⅛ teaspoon ground nutmeg or cloves
⅛ teaspoon cayenne pepper or ground dried chili of your choice
⅛ Pinch of kosher salt

Chop the chocolate into small pieces and put in a bowl. Combine the cream, sugar, nutmeg or cloves, cayenne, and salt in a saucepan and heat to just below a simmer. Remove from the heat and let stand for 5 minutes, or until the temperature drops to about 160°F.

Pour the cream over the chocolate and let stand for 2 minutes, then gently mix with a whisk or rubber spatula until combined and smooth.

PUT IT ALL TOGETHER

Toasts
Chocolate Sauce

Pour the chocolate sauce into a bowl, set it on a plate with the toasts, and have at it!

CHOCOLATE, CHEESE, *and* CHARRED BREAD

One day, I saw my friend and colleague Dara Tesser scooping up Camembert with a chunk of chocolate as if the chocolate were a cracker. She confessed that this was her favorite snack at home. I ruminated on that for a few days and came back with this recipe. Like many of my desserts, this one is finished with flaky salt. You may have an eccentric uncle who sends you red salt from Maui or smoked salt from Texas or rosemary salt from Napa. This is your chance to use it. There's no need for silverware, but do pass out extra napkins.

SOFTEN THE CHEESE

4 to 6 ounces Taleggio or other stinky soft cheese

Take the cheese out of the fridge 1 hour or so before serving. Remove the rind if you like, or leave it intact.

MAKE THE CHOCOLATE SAUCE

2 ounces dark chocolate (70% to 80% cacao)
½ cup heavy cream
½ teaspoon sugar
Pinch of kosher salt

Chop the chocolate into small pieces and put in a small bowl. Combine the cream, sugar, and salt in a small saucepan and heat to just below a simmer. Remove from the heat and let stand for 5 minutes, or until the temperature drops to about 160°F.

Pour the cream over the chocolate and let stand for 2 minutes, then gently stir with a whisk or rubber spatula until combined and smooth.

TEAR AND CHAR THE BREAD

⅓ baguette

The less finesse you bring to this dish, the better, so, using your hands, roughly pry open a baguette and tear it into comfortably dippable pieces (longer than they are wide). Turn a flame up high on your gas stove and, using tongs, hold the bread pieces one at a time right over the flame. The bread may catch on fire; that's okay. Let it burn a little, blow it out, and then burn it a little more. You're looking for the bread to be hot and with some charred spots here and there. It's a crude process, but it's fun to burn bread, and the char goes great with the chocolate. (If you don't have a gas stove, put the bread pieces on a baking sheet under a hot broiler. Check after a minute or too, to see if it's charred, then turn.)

PUT IT ALL TOGETHER

Softened cheese
Chocolate Sauce
Charred bread
¼ teaspoon flaky sea salt

Warm the cheese in a 300°F oven or toaster oven until it's gooey but not runny, about 3 minutes. Rewarm the chocolate sauce in a double boiler or in the microwave.

Smear the cheese over a plate—the result may be somewhere between a glob and a smear—whatever. Scatter the bread over the plate and drizzle the chocolate sauce all over. Finish with a sprinkling of salt.

WITH GRATITUDE

David Black, who willed this book to happen. Rux Martin, who got it 100 percent. Kathleen Hackett, who made sense of the recipes. Judith Sutton, who closely edited it. Melinda Kaminsky, who read everything again and again. Thanks to Max and Jimena Faerber for generously allowing us to take photographs (and crash!) in their lovely home. Chris Burunda, Stephanie Reagor, and Millicent Souris for helping get the times, weights, and temps right, as well as for adding some great ideas to the pot. To the staff of Houseman, past and present, for creating the time and space for this book to come into being. And to Dellapietras and Fish Tales, Cobble Hill's finest.

Peter Kaminsky

AFTERWORD

Like most New York City cooks, I've read and been influenced by Peter Kaminsky's broad inquiry into cooking and eating. Cooks who fish (I'm one of them) also know that Pete has made a fair dent in the literature of fishing. Not long after I opened Houseman, I came across Peter's *The Moon Pulled Up an Acre of Bass*, which is a rapturous tale about striped bass fishing off Montauk, Long Island. The book is visceral and personal, with lots of history and some really fun cooking to boot. What Pete makes isn't fancy. It's an informed cook making food for friends after a long day on the water.

I happened to be in the Union Square farmers' market the day Pete was coming in to Houseman and stopped to see if there was anything at Blue Moon Fish that I might offer him. Providentially, they had a couple of small weakfish. I bought them with confidence that the fisherman in Peter would go for a dish called Whole Weakfish, Slashed and Fried.

He did and, even better, he liked it. When he had finished eating, I came out and introduced myself. Not long thereafter, he returned to Houseman with his wife, Melinda. I don't remember what they ordered on that visit, but they must have liked it, because in mid-December, Peter called me at the restaurant. We chatted about the fall fishing season for a minute or two, and then he blew my mind by asking if I wanted to write a cookbook with him. I was floored and, like a fool, I set about to talk him out of it. He patiently waded through my objections and finally said, "Ned, it takes a long time to write a book." Truer words, as they say. That was 2015.

Ned Baldwin, Sept. 1, 2019

North Fork Egg Farm, LLC
The North Fork Egg Farm is located in Southold, NY.
As a small sustainable family farm, we have made the decision to not be certified organic. We know that we can provide the freshest and best quality eggs without having to go through a regulatory certification process.
Our hens are humanely raised. We release them from their coops early each morning to roam on pasture until dusk, when they return to their coops to sleep. The pasture they graze on has not been chemically treated with fertilizers or pesticides for over 10 years.
We feed our hens certified organic feed that is Non-GMO, chemical and pesticide free. We also supplement their feed with produce from our garden (which is chemical fertilizer and pesticide free as well) and occasionally with spent grain from a local brewery.
We feel that by following these principles, we provide our hens with a healthy and humane environment and provide you with fresh, high quality eggs at an affordable price.
Please feel free to contact us if you have questions or would like to visit our farm.

NOTE: Page references in *italics* indicate photographs.

A

B

C

D

I

L

M

N

O

P

Q

R

S

T

V

W

Y

Z